Christ-Centered Apologetics
Sharing the Gospel with Evidence

Joel Furches

CROSSLINK
PUBLISHING

Christ-Centered Apologetics: Sharing the Gospel with Evidence

꒡ CrossLink Publishing
꒢ www.crosslinkpublishing.com

ISBN 978-1-63357-000-9

Library of Congress Control Number: 2014940607

TABLE OF CONTENTS

FOREWORD

The conflict of ideas between biblical faith and pagan culture has gone on for millennia and its core has remained largely unchanged. Either reality, truth, and ethics are as the Bible states, or they derive from the imaginings of finite, fallen man aided by the deceptions of principalities and powers of this world-order. In the Old Testament times of ancient Israel the revealed supernatural cosmogony of Genesis radically clashed with the pagan naturalistic cosmology as expressed in *Enuma Elish* and other pagan writings. The same conflict occurred in the early centuries of Church history between Christians and Roman pagans. It was renewed between the sola scriptura authority of Protestantism and the subjective anthropocentricity of the so-called Enlightenment. Finally it continues in the post-Darwinian era today between what remains of biblical Christianity and the New Atheism.

As Joel Furches states, the New Atheism is far more evangelistic than older classical atheism and often appears very intimidating to believers whose understanding of the Word of God and its interpretation of the facts is shallow. Thankfully, the New Atheism repeats old arguments that have been answered repeatedly, projects a pretense of morality that hangs in mid-air like a magician's levitation act, often gets its facts backward, and is presuppositionally unaware of its own foundation. While accusing Christians of irrationality, the New Atheists commit logical blunders of their own. In trying to show that biblical religion conflicts with empirical evidences from historical science, archeology, historiography, and textual criticism, they seem to forget that the debate isn't over the facts. It's over the interpretation of the facts. Facts are mute. Facts alone don't speak for themselves. They are interpreted by their interpreters' worldviews.

Worldview discussions require comprehensive knowledge and skill often beyond that attainable by people educated only in a secularized, government-controlled system. But fruitful discussions between Christians and honestly seeking unbelievers can happen when they focus on specific straightforward questions. From his research on the kind of objections the New Atheists have popularized, Furches has assembled a mass of apologetic details with which to meet this challenge. He provides wise advice on when to question, when to listen, and when to talk. He gives the reader sample conversations to follow that help to avoid being endlessly diverted from the core of the gospel.

This volume stands in the tradition of empirical apologetics. It will guide the reader in dealing with the common and often ignorant conjectures thrown out in public conversation such as the supposed unreliability of the biblical text when other ancient books with far less textual evidence are casually accepted without question. This handy work ought to encourage believers that the Christian faith is rational, factually-based, and able to withstand the closest of examinations. Furches is to be commended for his emphasis on the centrality of the Lord Jesus Christ and His resurrection. After all, if faced with death with which historic religious leader would one want to converse about what lies beyond the grave?

Charles Clough, President
Biblical Framework Ministries
www.bibleframework.com

INTRODUCTION

I n September of 2001, a group of terrorists claiming connections to Islam hijacked and crashed several planes into key locations within the USA. This act had many repercussions, one of these being a kind of reactionary Atheism that has built to epidemic levels.

These so-called "New Atheists" differ from classical atheism in that they are aggressively evangelical and they believe that society can have morality without religion. Their argument is that religion promotes blind, irrational belief, and that such belief has led to the majority of atrocities throughout history, as reflected in slogans such as "Science flies us to the moon, religion flies us into buildings" (a direct reference to the events of 9/11).

This particular ideology has taken over the secular world by storm, essentially bullying anyone who dares to express religious beliefs out of the academic world, and making it extremely uncomfortable for nonacademics besides.

While this may seem to be a very bad thing for Christianity, it is arguably the best thing to happen to the Christian Church in the last century. The Church has been, and still is, in a state of lethargy and stagnation. The concepts that pass as theology and doctrine are deplorable, and the majority of people claiming to be Christian have no clear idea what that even means.

With the rise in aggressive antitheism has come a reactionary boom in Apologetics—the defense of Christian beliefs. The New Atheists are often more informed on the Bible, Christian doctrine, and history than most Christians, and present a challenge for Christians to step up their game and become schooled in their own faith.

Since the academic and science worlds are dominated by people who are outspoken opponents of religious beliefs, confrontations with these people can be intimidating indeed. However, it is important to remember that, while there is nothing fundamentally incompatible between Christianity and Science/ Philosophy, there *are* a number of things about reality that Christianity explains but Atheism does not:

1.) **Why there is something rather than nothing** - Try as they might, Atheists cannot explain how the universe came to be in the first place. There are no sufficient explanations for how something came from nothing without a timeless, spaceless, first-cause.

2.) **How life came from nonlife** - Even if one accepts that, over long periods of time, simpler life-forms can adapt and change into more complex life-forms, Atheists still have no sufficient explanation for how life could have arisen from more basic matter. There is no precedent for this, and the theories that claim to explain it are vague to say the least. Life forms appear to be more than simply mechanical systems operating on physics, like the solar system. They appear to have a consciousness and a will, things that are difficult to explain through material means.

3.) **Immaterial constructs** - Even if one gives up the concept of God, there are quite a few recognized immaterial things that one has to struggle with. Things such as thought, truth, logic, morality, purpose, and justice become a real problem if the universe is simply material. One could say that these things are imaginary, but then they would have to explain the immaterial construct of imagination.

No matter what Atheists throw out against theism, their system falls short of explaining these things. On the other hand, while these things are powerful arguments against Atheism, by themselves they do not argue for Christianity. They simply argue for some kind of nebulous, poorly defined deity. So what arguments should the Christian Apologist focus on?

The problem about engaging with any other worldview is that they typically want to object to every single thing that the Christian believes, from the origin of the universe, to the origin of life, to the historicity and reliability of the Bible, to miracles, to morality, to modern politics, and finally to Jesus himself.

There are two dangers of engaging on every single one of these topics. First, the argument never advances. It simply goes down a variety of rabbit trails but never arrives at any conclusions; and the opponent will simply keep digging up more arguments for the Christian to shoot down. Secondly (and worse), if Christians have to be right on every single one of these points in order to hold their faith, they may well find that they are wrong on one or more of their own preconceptions. If this is all it takes to lose their faith, Christians may find themselves doubting because of something that does not directly relate to the fundamentals of being a Christian.

For this reason, it is important to identify the nonnegotiables—that is, those things that, if proven false, would actually defeat Christianity. Once the Christian identifies these nonnegotiables, they may countenance all manner of arguments on the part of the Atheist—even if they have no good answers—saying, "Even if your argument is true, this remains the case."

From Apostle Paul onward, Christian evangelism has always focused on two things: Law and Gospel. That is to say that, in order to be considered "saved," a person must first recognize his or her own corruption and inadequacy, and repent of it. One must secondly place one's trust in Jesus rather than one's self. In order for these two concepts to remain intact, only two things have to be defended evangelically.

The first thing that must be defended is the fact that humans are corrupt and incapable of perfection. On classic Atheism, this is a problem because one must first prove some kind of transcendent moral standard that applies to everyone. Since the New Atheists have done the Christian Apologists the courtesy of arguing for a moral standard, this becomes much easier.

The second thing that must be defended is that Jesus rose bodily from the dead. This argument involves a defense of the New Testament documents and of historical facts related to the growth and advance of the Christian church.

By defending these two things, the Christian Apologist and Evangelist prove that all humans have a need, and that this need has been provided for.

Part I
DEFINING APOLOGETICS

Chapter 1
WHAT IS THE CHRISTIAN APOLOGIST'S AUDIENCE?

Ultimately, only God can remove people's blindness and rebellion and allow them to believe in Christ. That said, Christians are commanded not only to preach the gospel to all people, but to be prepared to give a defense for what they believe.

In commanding the Christian to give a defense[1], Apostle Peter is implying that the individual Christian should critically examine his or her beliefs to make certain that they are sound. This kind of self-inspection is repeatedly commended throughout the Bible: when the Bereans searched the scripture to confirm what Paul was preaching to them[2], when John instructs his readers to test the spirits[3] to see if they are from God, and when each of the apostles preached reasonable, evidential defenses for the Gospel they spread.

This is no less than the skeptical community calls upon a Christian to do. Christians are frequently and openly mocked for

---

[1] 1 Peter 3:15
[2] Acts 17:11
[3] 1 John 4:1

"just believing," and this is not entirely unjustified. If Christianity is in fact true, then it should hold up to the light of critical inspection. Looking at and answering Atheist objections to Christianity is healthy since it promotes self-inspection, which will ultimately refine a person's belief and give one reason to be confident in what he or she believes based on the fact that it holds up to criticism.

Consequently, the primary audience for Christian Apologetics should be other Christians. The bulk of Christians in the world have not deeply, critically considered their reasons for believing, with the result that they tend to hold a number of ungrounded and often damaging beliefs, and they are not able to defend what beliefs they hold.

These kinds of Christians tend to be the first to cave to the pressures of academic criticism and relinquish their beliefs when it appears to them that they have no reasonable defense. With Atheism becoming increasingly evangelical in nature, a vast number of Christians are forced to seek answers, and the seasoned Apologist must be available to give them.

The secondary audience for Apologetics should be unbelievers who are looking for answers. The most vocal members of any particular community, be it Atheist or Theist, tend to be the least interested in rational discussion of other's views. But just because there are plenty of loudmouths more interested in talking than in listening does not mean that there aren't those who have an interest in discussing ideas and considering alternatives. For many of these people, Christianity seems unreasonable because no one has ever given them reasons, just a vague plea to "have faith."

For this reason, it is incumbent upon the Christian to be willing to listen as well as to talk. If Christians want to share their worldview and reasoning with others, they should be willing to pay others the same courtesy. This practice gives the Christian the ability to understand what questions and objections the non-Christian may have, and to address these concerns. If Christianity is true, then the Christian should have no reason to fear hearing alternative ideas. If Christianity is false, then a Christian would be hypocritical not to pursue the truth.

Christians who spend all or most of their time arguing with entrenched Atheists are doing neither themselves nor the Atheist any good. If the person is clearly uninterested in even considering any answers to their objections or countenancing any alternatives to their worldview, then the discussion becomes nothing more than a shouting match, each person trying to tout their position more loudly than the other.

Three types of Apologetics:

-External:

External Apologetics focus on evangelism. The primary purpose of Apologetics to those external to the church is to remove intellectual objections to the faith. We live in a culture where it is the common belief that "faith" is the opposite of "reason." It is not surprising, then, that most nonbelievers think that Christianity is unreasonable. They believe that science answers all the questions of the universe and that religion is for those who need some kind of false hope or comfort.

External Apologetics exist for this kind of person. If it can be shown that not only is Christianity reasonable, but that it is not opposed to science, and is the best model for reality, then this opens the doors for people to accept the truth of Christian belief.

Evangelism is not exclusive to emotional pleas of a person's testimony or the loving diligence of a believer in the life of an unbeliever (although these things are certainly important and effective). There are plenty of examples of people coming to Christ because of the persuasiveness of a logical, coherent argument for the truthfulness of scripture and the gospel. C.S. Lewis' *Mere Christianity*[1] has been effective in many people's lives, as an example.

External Apologetics can, however, become a trap of arguing with those who are vehemently opposed to the truth of Christianity and whose only concern is to discredit the faith. Arguments should never be directed at people, merely at ideas, which leads to the second kind of Apologetics:

-Internal:

Internal Apologetics are equally important to external. These are Apologetic arguments for the sake of the believer. These types of arguments address particular concerns that may be stumbling blocks to thoughtful believers, causing them to doubt their faith.

In many Christian circles, the importance of Apologetics within the Church is underestimated. Many Christians live in a semi-isolated environment where all of their family, friends, and social activities are largely with other Christians. Consequently, they are unprepared for the aggressive skepticism and vitriolic hatred directed at Christian beliefs, especially from academic circles.

As a result of this, many young people from Christian families who receive secular educations, especially at the college level, fall away from the faith because they do not know that there are answers to these questions, and under the assault of a skeptical world, Christian beliefs seem flimsy at best. A Christian that does not take into account the hard questions about science and the accuracy of the Bible, in the words of Christ, "has no root in himself, but endures for a while, and when tribulation or persecution arises on account of the word, immediately he falls away." (Matthew 13:21, ESV)

-Lateral:

"Lateral" Apologetics deal with false teachings within the Church that could lead to errors in doctrine, bad practices, and false religion. We will not focus on this kind of Apologetics in this book. Good pastoral leadership and a diligent reading of scripture are the most important tools in this kind of Apologetic.

A word about being wrong:

It is important that Christians understand that it is possible to be mistaken about something they hold to be an important part of their faith without their entire belief system collapsing.

Whatever beliefs you hold, you must have good reasons, not just justifications, for why you hold them. A well-supported faith based on solid reasoning is much less easily shaken than one that is unsupported or unsupportable.

Chapter 2
THE FOCUS OF EXTERNAL APOLOGETICS

The Higgs-Boson particle was an object proposed by theoretical physicists to explain why objects have mass. These physicists looked at the property of mass mathematically, and predicted that the best explanation for it was a field of yet-to-be-discovered, subatomic particles that gave the property of mass to other particles that moved through this field.

This is how science works. Scientists observe reality, and then form theories to explain why various things act the way they do. A good theory will predict how reality will act in any given circumstance.

Later, experimental physicists were able to detect the existence of the Higgs-Boson particle by use of a supercollider. The theory proved to be sound because it correctly predicted the results of the experiment.

In order for a worldview to be correct, the predictions it makes must match the reality we observe.

The worldview of Christianity explains a great many things that would be difficult to explain otherwise:

1.)   Why something exists rather than nothing

Some of the prominent atheistic arguments for the existence of a material universe include redefining "nothing" as a quantum vacuum or denying that "nothing" was ever a state. The problem with the first argument is that a quantum vacuum is "something," not "nothing." The problem with the second argument is time. Time cannot extend forever into the past, and even attempts to get around this, such as the multiverse theory, are ad hoc solutions and involve an infinite regression, which is logically inconsistent.

Since God exists in an eternal state outside of time, his existence is consistent with time and space, provides a robust explanation for the existence of time and space, and is evidenced by the other arguments in this series

2.)   Why the universe appears to have specified complexity that is fine-tuned for the existence of life on earth

Positing a mindless, unguided, and random expansion of space and time does not explain why this expansion did not collapse in upon itself at the moment it began or expand so rapidly that it dispersed entirely. The rate of expansion is so exact that it is massively improbable.

The size of the sun, the exact positioning of the earth, the protective gravitational vacuum provided by the outer planets, and the exact chemical mix for life on earth is also astoundingly improbable.

Arguments for a mindless universe that just happens to support life include the anthropic principle—the idea that infinite realities exist simultaneously and humans just happen to live in the one that supports life, so of course they think they are designed—and the somewhat weak argument that, while it was improbable, it still happened.

Intelligent design provides a very reasonable explanation for apparent design.

3.) **Why human beings are capable of complex reasoning, emotions, love, art, language, and other sophisticated thoughts that are not evidenced in any other known life form to the same degree**

Once again, it is difficult to start from the premise of mindless evolution and end with the idea that humans are anything more than organisms bent on preserving and passing on their DNA. The fact that humans not only pursue art, philosophy, and science, but also exult in those things *more* than reproduction cannot easily be explained through materialism.

Antitheism would have to explain how such pursuits are adaptive and the logical result of mindless evolution *and* how humans are capable of dominating all other species on the planet in order to be consistent.

The Christian concept that humans were created in the image of God explains not only these pursuits, but explains the quality of these pursuits as superior to mere reproduction.

Humans do not simply seek to reproduce, they seek to create legacy.

4.) **Why human beings are capable of such depths of depravity not evidenced in the same degree in any other life form**

Atheism will appeal to psychology and sociology to explain human behavior, which is legitimate, but what explains human psychology? Atheism can only find explanatory power in evolution such that the mind is—paradoxically—a mindless organ that is forced to act according to its chemistry and cannot act otherwise.

The fact that humans are capable of recognizing depravity in others, are offended by it, seek to reform it, feel guilt, and are capable of redemptive behavior all speak against this explanation.

The fact that humans are capable of meta-cognition—thinking about thinking—and are therefore able to postulate their own mindlessness is counterintuitive to say the least.

Christianity perfectly explains the dualistic nature of humans *and* presents a solution.

5.)   **The existence of morality**

Atheist philosophy will appeal to utilitarianism in order to explain morality. That is to say that morality is that which best promotes the well-being of individuals and the community to the maximum degree. Nuances of morality, such as sexual preferences and dietary restrictions, atheists will say relate to culture and are dispensable.

What this philosophy fails to explain is motivation. If the ultimate end of an individual is death, what obligation does that person have to promote community? Why not simply live a life of selfish hedonism in order to gain the most enjoyable life possible?

On the other hand, if the preservation and evolution of the human race is of ultimate importance, why not adopt Hitler's approach and expedite the process by forcibly eliminating inferior people from the gene pool?

On atheism, there is no motivation to classic morality besides some baseless feeling of goodwill.

Pantheistic religions deny the existence of morality entirely—stating that it is an illusion—while paradoxically embracing a system of karma that insists the individual suffer away their bad deeds.

On Christianity, however, morality is defined by God's nature. Since God created the universe, anything that does not serve the purpose for which it was created is purposeless. Rather than insisting that humans attempt to live up to God's expectations outside of God's nature—as religions such as Islam and Mormonism do—Christianity provides a system wherein the individual surrenders self-will in exchange for imputed perfection. This is the only system of morality that is entirely consistent.

6.)   The existence of evil

The existence of evil is probably the most common argument against Christian theism. There are two reasons that this argument does not work.

The first reason is that, in order to have evil, one must first have a standard against which to judge good and evil. By admitting to evil, the skeptic is admitting to a standard that they intuitively recognize, which is evidence *for* theism.

The second reason is that the problem of evil is the question around which Christianity is built. Briefly stated, Christianity is the belief that God created a universe in which free-will creatures existed. These creatures chose to act selfishly, seeking to exult themselves to the exclusion of the very God upon which they depended. This resulted in a situation wherein God's nature demanded two seemingly contradictory things. His justice demanded punishment and elimination of evil, while his love demanded mercy, forgiveness, and compassion. These two demands were met in the actions of Jesus Christ. By taking the punishment for sins, God's justice was appeased, and by offering forgiveness to those who asked for it, God's love was appeased. The existence of evil thereby exults God's nature by allowing God to act out his attributes to their fullest extent.

God's response to evil confirms his nature and is fully consistent with reality.

7.)   The existence of transcendent, immaterial things such as logic and math.

Logic and math define the universe. But in order to have a definition, something must have a definer.

Atheism will argue that humans simply observe the universe and in observing, they define it.

However the universe existed prior to humans, and the math and logic that define it must therefore also exist exterior to humans. It gets more complicated than that, however. Math and Logic are immaterial constructs. They do not exist in the material universe, they must exist in a mind. Since the universe existed prior to humans, something had to exist prior to the universe in order to define it. That the universe is defined by a definer exterior and prior *to* the universe is consistent and explanatory.

In order to be valid, any other worldview must be able to adequately explain all of these facts in a unified way.

A skeptic named John Wisdom tells this story:

> "Two people return to their long neglected garden and find, among the weeds, that a few of the old plants are surprisingly vigorous. One says to the other, 'It must be that a gardener has been coming and doing something about these weeds.' The other disagrees and an argument ensues. They pitch their tents and set a watch. No gardener is ever seen. The believer wonders if there is an invisible gardener, so they patrol with bloodhounds but the bloodhounds never give a cry. Yet the believer remains unconvinced, and insists that the gardener is invisible, has no scent, and gives no sound. The skeptic doesn't agree, and asks how a so-called invisible, intangible, elusive gardener differs from an imaginary gardener, or even no gardener at all."

One complaint that skeptics have with the concept of God is that there is no evidence they can supply or test that they could apply that would falsify God's existence. Anything they can supply to show that God does not exist simply causes the theist to redefine their God. If they were to prove that life evolved from nonlife, the Theist would simply say that this is how God chose to bring life about. If they show that the evil in the world does not support the concept of a good and loving God, the Theist will say that God has his reasons for doing so. So how does an invisible, intangible, elusive God differ from an imaginary God, or even no God at all?

If God remains invisible, intangible and elusive, then this remains a problem. Thankfully for the Christian, there is a concrete answer. Because the Christian's God took on flesh and became a real person in real history.

Moreover, he performed a real miracle that impacted the entire world. If skeptics want to falsify the Christian God, they have concrete evidence that they can examine.

This is one of two reasons that External Apologetics—that is, apologetics aimed at speaking to unbelievers—should focus on the life, death, and resurrection of Jesus, and on the reliability of the New Testament. Verify this and the Christian God is proven. Falsify this and God may exist, but he is not the Christian God.

The second reason that External Apologetics should focus on the life, death, and resurrection of Jesus is that ultimately, External Apologetics serves the purpose of evangelism. If External Apologetics is made to serve any other purpose—to win an argument or prove one's intellectual superiority, for instance—it is a waste of time and a disservice to whomever it is directed. External Apologetics should be used by a Christian only as a means of answering troubling questions for unbelievers and removing obstacles to them accepting faith.

With this in mind, it is important to remember that one of the greatest obstacles to people believing in Christ, and one of the best evidences one can present to the truthfulness of Christianity, is the life of the believer.

Chapter 3
THE BEST APOLOGETIC

C hristianity is a faith that, properly understood, stands on the shoulders of the humble and unassuming. For every loud-mouthed media hound waving a bible and making Christians seem foolish, there are thousands more that serve quietly and humbly behind the scenes.

One of the fundamental tenets of Christianity is that it is supposed to change the believer. If one professes to believe in Christ and his teachings, but acts no differently from the time when they were an unbeliever, their claim looks suspicious at best.

The best apologetic is a life well-lived. One of the main reasons that Jesus is such an intriguing figure to all people-groups the world over is that his life was lived so purely. Even the most ardent atheist must admit that he was "a great moral teacher."

On the flip side, one poor choice can utterly ruin the testimony of the most well-intentioned apologist.

In the twenty-third psalm, the Psalmist says, "He leads me in paths of righteousness for His name's sake." (Psalms 23:3 ESV) What the Psalmist is saying here is that God directs His followers to purity because they are representatives of Him. They reflect His name and reputation, and so He is concerned that they do not stray.

While Christianity is not a faith where the followers must do good deeds to earn merit, it *is* a faith where good deeds are the measurement of a person's alignment. The scriptures teach over and over that true followers will bear fruits that mark them as children of God.

While not all people have the ability and training to expound upon their faith, *everyone* who is Christian can produce fruits. A poorly educated person who is unable to make a verbal defense for his faith, through living out the Christian life in a faultless way, may do more to redeem those around him than the most silver-tongued theologian.

While most Apologists will appeal to 1Peter 3:15 in order to justify Apologetics, taken in the larger context, that passage says this:

1 Peter 3:8-17
English Standard Version (ESV)

Suffering for Righteousness' Sake

[8] Finally, all of you, have unity of mind, sympathy, brotherly love, a tender heart, and a humble mind. [9] Do not repay evil for evil or reviling for reviling, but on the contrary, bless, for to this you were called, that you may obtain a blessing. [10] For

"Whoever desires to love life and see good days, let him keep his tongue from evil and his lips from speaking deceit; [11] let him turn away from evil and do good; let him seek peace and pursue it. [12] For the eyes of the Lord are on the righteous, and his ears are open to their prayer. But the face of the Lord is against those who do evil."

[13] Now who is there to harm you if you are zealous for what is good? [14] But even if you should suffer for righteousness' sake, you will be blessed. Have no fear of them, nor be troubled, [15] but in your hearts honor Christ the Lord as holy, always being prepared to make a defense to anyone who asks you for a reason for the hope that is in you; yet do it with gentleness and respect, [16] having a good conscience, so that, when you are slandered, those who revile your good behavior in Christ may be put to shame. [17] For it is better to suffer for doing good, if that should be God's will, than for doing evil.

What Peter defines here is true apologetics. Not simply well-reasoned argumentation, but well-enacted living.

Part II
THE EVIDENCE FOR CHRIST

Chapter 4
THE RELIABILITY OF THE NEW TESTAMENT DOCUMENTS

In Carl Sagan's signature work, *Cosmos*[2], the author and scientist famously coined the "Sagan Standard," which states that "Extraordinary claims require extraordinary evidence." This quote was in reference to the Judeo-Christian belief in a personal God. Essentially, Sagan was saying that since any claims regarding God refer to the transcendent, immaterial universe, the usual standards of proof were insufficient to address such issues. Sagan himself did not suggest what sort of proof might be considered adequate to speak to religious claims, which leaves the question wide open.

Most skeptics who subscribe to the "Sagan Standard" would further suggest that no such evidence exists, and then neatly conclude that either the transcendent doesn't exist, or that if it does, nothing about it can be known. Either conclusion would exclude religion entirely, since *every* religion makes some sort of statement about the nature of the transcendent.

In a way, this intentionally stacks the deck against someone who is attempting to make the case for any religious claim. Since religious claims require extraordinary evidence, and extraordinary evidence is left undefined, then any evidence the Apologist presents can simply be said not to be sufficiently extraordinary and therefore dismissed.

The Bible does, in fact, set a standard for extraordinary evidence. When sent to Egypt to free his people, Moses said to God, "But behold, they will not believe me or listen to my voice, for they will say, 'The Lord did not appear to you.'"(Exodus 4:1 ESV). This is an instance in which Moses was making an extraordinary claim and expected not to be believed. God responds by telling Moses when he throws down his staff, it will turn into a serpent. This is the extraordinary evidence to support the extraordinary claim.

This pattern is repeated throughout the Bible. More often than not, when a message came from God, that message was accompanied with a miraculous sign. In fact, this pattern continues until the entire canon of scripture is complete. The apostles continued to miraculously heal people, cast out demons, and prophesy about the future long after Christ was gone from earth. These miraculous deeds lent authority to their message, which ultimately became the text of scripture.

Christ himself used the same standard of evidence when he told his own skeptics "If I am not doing the works of my Father, then do not believe me; but if I do them, even though you do not believe me, believe the works, that you may know and understand that the Father is in me and I am in the Father" (John 10:37-38 ESV). The works in this instance refer not only to the miraculous deeds that Jesus performed on a regular basis, but also the purity of these deeds and of his teaching.

Christ claimed to be God - an extraordinary claim if ever there was one. When asked to support this claim, his response was this: "Just as Jonah was three days and three nights in the belly of the great fish, so will the son of man be three days and three nights in the heart of the earth" (Matthew 12:40 ESV) Jesus gave his resurrection as the ultimate proof for his claims.

Throughout scripture, miraculous events were almost exclusively performed in order to lend authority to some message that was from God, culminating in the resurrection of Christ: the final proof for the final message from God. In this way, scripture seems to support the Sagan Standard. It offers extraordinary proof for its extraordinary claims. While miracles are certainly awesome and impressive, the truly extraordinary claim is that God communicates with humans, and the miracles are subservient to that message.

But herein lies a problem. If miracles are the extraordinary proofs, they, too, are extraordinary in their own right. The Sagan Standard would demand extraordinary evidence for the miracles. But any extraordinary evidence would, itself, be miraculous, and therefore require proof. This is an infinite regression of the extraordinary that never satisfies the skeptical mindset. The Sagan Standard is a trap from which no supernatural, miraculous, or transcendent claim may escape. By saying that the extraordinary must be evidenced by the extraordinary, nothing ever gets explained at all.

Nor do Christian Apologists necessarily agree with the Sagan Standard. If the evidence is conclusive, why must it be any more unusual than evidence for any other claim? Since we cannot have any *direct evidence* (live eyewitnesses that can be interviewed) of the life of Christ, we have to rely on *circumstantial evidence*—that is, indirect clues in the form of archeological data, historical accounts, and written testimonies from that time period. Any one of these forms of evidence is not conclusive. Instead, one must take *all the pieces* of evidence combined and see which conclusion is most likely to match all of the evidence.

The documents that compose the New Testament are the primary link that modern Christians have to the teachings of Jesus and the apostles. Consequently, they are under a great deal of attack from every non-Christian faction.

Although the inerrancy of scripture is an important topic for Internal Apologetics, for the purposes of External Apologetics, it is not necessary to prove that the documents we possess be 100 percent accurate in order for Christianity to be true. We would only need the documents to transmit sufficient evidence that:

- Jesus was a real, historical person
- Jesus claimed to be God
- The first century church contained a number of people who claimed to be eyewitnesses of a resurrected Jesus
- That early Christians believed that salvation comes through a repentance of sin and an acceptance of the redemptive work of Jesus Christ.

In order to discuss this subject, there are a number of factors to take into consideration. In the next several chapters, we will discuss evidence that:

1.) The documents were authored within decades of the events they record
2.) The authors were either eyewitnesses or had access to eyewitness accounts
3.) The documents have been transmitted accurately to the present day

Chapter 5
How Close to the Events Were the Documents?

Most non-Christians who speak to the subject of the date of the original documents will tend to place the dating of those documents fairly late: as much as two centuries after the events to which they refer. In so doing, they can argue that Jesus of Nazareth and his legacy was greatly exaggerated due to a mythology that had built up about him in the century before anything was written about him. Although in the ancient world, memorizing and passing on accounts orally was a common practice, and just because the events referenced in the books are two hundred years out of date does not mean that they got the essential detail (the resurrection) wrong.

That said, there is a decent amount of evidence that the New Testament documents were written early.

Destruction of the Second Temple

The book of Ezra tells of the rebuilding of the Jewish Temple after Solomon's original Temple was destroyed by the Babylonians. While Ezra completed his Temple around 518 BCE, Herod the Great

(74 BCE) reconstructed this temple from the ground up. During the construction and expansion of the temple, worship continued[3]. This construction was evidently still going on during the time of Jesus, as the disciples pointed out to him in Matthew 24.

In CE 66, a massive Jewish rebellion broke out in Jerusalem against the Roman Empire. Rome responded in CE 70 by sieging Jerusalem, and then sacking and destroying Herod's Temple[4]. This siege and sacking constituted a brutal bloodbath in Jerusalem and is an event mourned to this day by Jews in a yearly event called Tisha B'Av[5].

Oddly, this event is never mentioned in the epistles. Jesus seems to prophesy Jerusalem's destruction (Mark 13:2, Matthew 24, and Luke 19) four decades before it happened. If this is truly what these verses refer to, why didn't any of the New Testament books affirm that Jesus' prophecy had come true?

In fact, with the destruction of the Temple and the sacking of Jerusalem by Rome being the most devastating event in the first century, how is it that there is not a single reference to it anywhere in the New Testament books?

One possible explanation is that the books were written before this event, which would place their writing somewhere within five decades of the events to which they refer, early enough that eyewitnesses would still be available, and certainly before a large mythology built up around it.

The Death of Paul, Peter, and James

It is indisputable that the three most influential people in the early church (or at the very least, the New Testament record) were Apostle Peter, the most vocal of Jesus' original disciples, Apostle Paul, the most prolific writer in the New Testament, and James the brother of Jesus, who was the leader of the core church in Jerusalem. James was martyred in the city of Jerusalem in CE 62[6], Apostle Paul was martyred in Rome in CE 64, and Peter was martyred in CE 65[7]. Not only does Paul's official historian, Luke, fail to mention any of their deaths in his book of Acts, but none of the Epistles, including John's and James's, mention the death of either. One would assume that if any of these books were late forgeries, they would have capitalized on mentioning the well-known martyrdoms of these well-known and revered apostles.

The Order in which Luke's books were written

Luke makes it clear in the preface to his book of Acts that this is a sequel to his Gospel (Acts 1:1-3). Clearly, the Gospel of Luke is written prior to the book of Acts. Since, as mentioned above, the book of Acts probably predates the death of James in CE 62, this means that the information that Luke has about Jesus' life and ministry and the information that he passed on in his Gospel may well date within forty years of Jesus' death.

Paul's citation of New Testament scripture

In his first letter to Timothy, written around CE 64, Paul writes this:

> **1 Timothy 5:17-18**
> English Standard Version (ESV)
>
> [17] Let the elders who rule well be considered worthy of double honor, especially those who labor in preaching and teaching. [18] For the Scripture says, "You shall not muzzle an ox when it treads out the grain," and, "The laborer deserves his wages."

In this passage Paul quotes two scriptures. The first scripture he quotes is "You shall not muzzle an ox when it treads out the grain." This is a passage from Deuteronomy 25:4. The second, "The laborer deserves his wages," is from Luke 10:7.

The fact that Paul is quoting the writings of his contemporary, Luke, as gospel, is a strong indication that Luke had already written his gospel by this time, CE 64, and that Paul already acknowledges it as authoritative scripture.

Another example of this is Paul's quotation of Luke's account of the Last Supper. In Luke 22:19-20, the Beloved Physician writes:

Luke 22:19-20
English Standard Version (ESV)

[19] And he took bread, and when he had given thanks, he broke it and gave it to them, saying, "This is my body, which is given for you. Do this in remembrance of me." [20] And likewise the cup after they had eaten, saying, "This cup that is poured out for you is the new covenant in my blood.

Paul echoes this account almost exactly in 1 Corinthians 11:23-25, which says:

1 Corinthians 11:23-25
English Standard Version (ESV)

[23] For I received from the Lord what I also delivered to you, that the Lord Jesus on the night when he was betrayed took bread, [24] and when he had given thanks, he broke it, and said, "This is my body which is for you. Do this in remembrance of me." [25] In the same way also he took the cup, after supper, saying, "This cup is the new covenant in my blood. Do this, as often as you drink it, in remembrance of me."

Paul's summary of the Gospel

Higher criticism/form criticism is the practice of examining in detail the use of words, writing styles, themes, and content of a text in order to reconstruct its historical origin. This method does not take a text at face value, but rather assumes that the text has been significantly altered over time. According to form critics, several of the books attributed to Paul were forgeries by later authors capitalizing on Paul's renown in order to sell their ideas.

That said, even the most liberal critics will agree that Romans, First and Second Corinthians, and Galatians, were probably written by Paul of Tarsus[8].

In 1 Corinthians 15:3-8 (written between CE 53 and 57[9]), Paul wrote this:

1 Corinthians 15:3-8
English Standard Version (ESV)

[3] For I delivered to you as of first importance what I also received: that Christ died for our sins in accordance with the Scriptures, [4] that he was buried, that he was raised on the third day in accordance with the Scriptures, [5] and that he appeared to Cephas, then to the twelve. [6] Then he appeared to more than five hundred brothers at one time, most of whom are still alive, though some have fallen asleep. [7] Then he appeared to James, then to all the apostles. [8] Last of all, as to one untimely born, he appeared also to me.

What Paul summarizes here is the essential events of the Gospel, the bare bones of what has to be true in order for Christianity to be an accurate worldview. This was written within three decades of the events to which it refers, and it perfectly correlates with the events described in the four Gospels, lending credence to their accuracy and early dating.

More than this, however, Paul makes the claim that many of the hundreds of witnesses to the resurrected Jesus were still alive.

This appears to be a statement intended to relay the accuracy of what he is writing. Paul is saying, "ask the eyewitnesses. Many of them are still among us." If this statement were untrue, it seems unlikely that the church would have preserved the writings of someone who is obviously bluffing.

Paul apparently got at least some of this information from Peter and James, and in Galatians (written in the mid-fifties[9]), he identifies his meeting with these disciples as having been fourteen years prior to the writing of the letter to the Galatians:

Galatians 1:15-19
English Standard Version (ESV)

[15] But when he who had set me apart before I was born, and who called me by his grace, [16] was pleased to reveal his Son to me, in order that I might preach him among the Gentiles, I did not immediately consult with anyone; [17] nor did I go up to Jerusalem to those who were apostles before me, but I went away into Arabia, and returned again to Damascus.

[18] Then after three years I went up to Jerusalem to visit Cephas and remained with him fifteen days. [19] But I saw none of the other apostles except James the Lord's brother.

Galatians 2:1
English Standard Version (ESV)

2 Then after fourteen years I went up again to Jerusalem with Barnabas, taking Titus along with me.

Most scholars place Paul's conversion somewhere between CE 33 and 36[10]. If true, this passage in Galatians allows us to estimate that Paul spoke face-to-face with eyewitnesses to Jesus' life, death, and resurrection within five years of those events.

Luke's citation of other Gospels

In previous points, we have shown that:

- The book of Acts was authored *after* the book of Luke
- The book of Acts fails to mention the death of Paul, Peter, and James
- The book of Acts fails to mention the destruction of the temple
- Paul cites what appear to be passages from the Gospel of Luke in his letters to Timothy (CE 64), and the Corinthians (CE 57)

All of these factors lend strong support to the idea that Luke's Gospel was written fairly early. Consequently, it is telling to see that Luke's Gospel appears to draw heavily upon the Gospels of Matthew and Mark for source material. Luke's Gospel contains whole passages that appear to have been copied from Matthew and Mark's Gospels. The Gospel of Luke contains 350 verses from Mark and 250 verses from Matthew[11].

In the introduction to his Gospel, Luke makes no secret of the fact that he is simply retelling the events of Jesus' life that he was not directly witness to. He also states that his object is to tell the story in an orderly and organized manner (Luke 1:1-4). It is not surprising, then, that he is drawing upon other source material. If we can date Luke's Gospel early because of the above-stated facts, and Luke appears to be quoting Matthew and Mark, then it is reasonable to believe that Matthew and Mark's Gospels' were written even earlier.

Chapter 6
Do the Documents Contain Eyewitness Accounts?

Proverbs 18:17
English Standard Version (ESV)

[17] The one who states his case first seems right, until the other comes and examines him.

Both those who attempt to prove the accuracy of the Biblical accounts and those who try to discredit them have an agenda. There are likely no neutral parties in this debate.

The attempts to discredit the Gospels have been exceptionally thorough, examining every possible flaw or contradiction.

This has forced the Christian Scholars to become extraordinarily detailed in their defense of these scriptures.

Anyone examining these scriptures has both the prosecuting attacks and the defenses to these attacks to examine and determine which argument seems most reasonable.

It is important to realize that there are no new arguments against the authenticity of the New Testament. The arguments that exist are continually rehashed. On the other hand, scholarship and archeology keep unearthing more and more evidence from the time period in which the Gospels were written that supports their authenticity.

The four Gospels claim to tell the events and teachings of Jesus. In order to trust these accounts, it would have to be shown that they accurately reflect what people witnessed Jesus do and heard Jesus say.

One of the things that support the idea that the Gospels get their information from eyewitnesses is the consistency of all four gospels. For instance:

- There are not a wide variety of Christ legends from the first century. Simply the four Gospels that all harmonize in the important details
- There are no counter traditions that contradict the Gospels on any major points such as how and where Jesus lived, ministered, died and rose.
- There are no counter Gospels that set the story in other places, or contradict the core theology, or change any of the major characters
- Jesus is consistently surrounded by twelve core disciples and three close disciples. He always dies in Jerusalem at the hands of the Romans through the machinations of the religious leaders of Israel and is resurrected three days later, etc.

The enormous consistency of the Gospels and the lack of a vast library of "Jesus Legends" cropping up over time belie the liberal claim that Jesus is largely mythologized. Let's take a look at each particular book.

Matthew

The book of Matthew doesn't actually claim authorship anywhere in the book. The church fathers (the second and third generation of church leaders who followed the apostles) credited the disciple Matthew as the author[12]. It seems unlikely that this was an intentional deception. Anyone forging a document and crediting it to a disciple of Jesus would most likely have chosen to credit it to one of the more high-profile disciples like Peter, James, or John. Matthew is an odd choice to falsely credit with authorship, especially since he was a former tax collector for Rome, and thus a traitor to the Jews.

If the church fathers were correct, and Matthew was the author, then the contents of this book are mostly eyewitness accounts to the events.

Mark

John Mark, who is credited with writing the Gospel of Mark was not, so far as we can tell, an actual witness to the life of Christ (tradition states that he was the young man who left his cloak and fled naked from the scene of Jesus' arrest in *Mark* 14:52) [13]. John Mark was mentioned in the book of *Acts* as someone who accompanied Peter and Paul on their various journeys (Acts 12:12, 12:25, 15:37). The church fathers credited John Mark with transcribing Peter's account of Jesus' life[14]. If this is true, then the Gospel of Mark was essentially Peter's notes on Jesus' life as transcribed by Mark.

Luke

The Gospel of Luke more or less says up front that it is more of a biography than an eyewitness account of Jesus' life (Luke 1:1-4). Clearly, Luke and Acts have the same author as shown by the prefaces and writing styles of both books. Luke is credited as author because in the book of Acts, he occasionally slips into the first person plural (we) when describing events that Luke was present for. So it's an inference of scholars that Luke must have written Acts and Luke[15].

Luke doesn't describe how he came by the information contained in his Gospel. Much of what Luke records is copied almost verbatim from Matthew and Mark[11], which indicates that he leaned heavily on these sources. Additionally, Luke contains a great deal of information that appears to be from the perspective of Mary (Jesus' mother). This includes the visitation of Gabriel to Mary announcing her pregnancy (Luke 1:19) and the events surrounding the birth and childhood of Jesus (Luke 2); events that the other Gospels do not record. This has led many to speculate that Luke interviewed Mary for some of these details (they may also have come from James, Jesus' brother).

John

Like all of the gospels, John does not say outright that he is the author of his book; however, every time John speaks of himself in the book, he doesn't use his name, but rather calls himself "the disciple that Jesus loved," which scholars take to be an obvious indication that he, John, was the author[16].

Of all the gospels, John's comes under the heaviest attack by scholars for several reasons. First of all, John's Gospel contains a variety of accounts and details that are not found in the other books. Secondly, John appears to have what is called a "High Christology" as compared to the other gospels. This means that (critics say) John's gospel reflects a more refined doctrine that casts Christ as God incarnate and spells out the sacrificial death of Jesus for the sins of mankind in a way that the other gospels don't[17]. Because John does these things, critics believe it was written much later when the church's theology had evolved to the point where this is what they believed and taught.

As a result of these criticisms, most skeptics will write off any evidence one might draw from the book of John as being the product of a forged gospel rather than an eyewitness.

There is very little doubt that the book of John *was* written well after the other Gospels, but the church fathers tell us that the disciple John was

1.)   Much younger than the other apostles, probably just a teenager when he followed Jesus[18]
2.)   Lived well into his nineties[19]
3.)   Did most of his writing late in life[20].

If true, this would account for the differences seen between John's gospel and the earlier gospels. John could well have been aware of the other gospels, and written his to "fill in the gaps," so to speak - clarifying some things about Jesus life and teachings that may have become concerns in the early church. If this is so, then John would have highlighted aspects of Jesus life and ministry that the others had not in order to address the specific questions that the early church was raising.

In the next several chapters, we will take a detailed look at the eyewitness nature of the accounts given in these documents.

Chapter 7
EVIDENCE FOR THE BOOK OF *MATTHEW*

The book of Matthew is quoted by early Christian writers (as early as CE 110) and is quoted more frequently than Mark or Luke[21]. As mentioned before, tradition strongly indicates the disciple Matthew as the author of this gospel. In fact, there is not a single tradition that even suggests that anyone *but* Matthew authored the book. In every single manuscript copy available for this book, going back as early as 125 years after Christ, Matthew is credited for authorship[21]. The author of Matthew does not identify himself in the text of the book. This makes it improbable that someone forged the Gospel and then attributed it to one of Jesus' disciples. Even if they did, Matthew is a very odd choice if the author wanted to lend credibility to a forgery. Matthew, a former tax collector for Rome (Matthew 10:3), would be the very last disciple anyone would credit for a gospel written primarily to a Jewish audience (as we will soon see, the Gospel of Matthew is just that). In this instance, the fact that the author does not identify himself tends to dismiss the idea that it was a late forgery.

Papias of Hierapolis was a bishop in the early church. He lived about 100 years after Christ and wrote a great deal about the oral traditions of the apostles and the early church. While none of Papias' actual writings have survived, he was quoted extensively by other writers, allowing us to construct a decent amount of his writings. Papias is quoted as saying "Instead [of writing in Greek], Matthew arranged the oracles in the Hebrew dialect, and each man interpreted them as he was able.[22]"

This quote indicates that Matthew did write something (although all of the available copies of *Matthew* are written in Greek)[21].

Irenaeus was bishop of Lugdunum and an early apologist for Christianity. He wrote around 150 years after Christ, and was quoted as saying, "Now Matthew published also a book of the Gospel among the Hebrews in their own dialect, while Peter and Paul were preaching the gospel in Rome and founding the Church" (Eusebius, *HE* 5.8.2.). This quote tells us that what Matthew wrote, he wrote for a Jewish audience. This correlates with what we know of the Gospel of Matthew, since this Gospel in particular heavily references Old Testament prophecies and parallels with the apparent purpose of convincing the reader that Jesus was, indeed, the prophesied Messiah.

This quote also tells us that Matthew wrote something during the time that Peter and Paul were in Rome.

Eusebius (CE 263 – 339), Saint Jerome (CE 347 – 420), Augustine of Hippo (CE 354 – 430), and other early writers all mention Matthew as authoring something about Christ[21].

There is a great deal of evidence within the book of Matthew that the author was Jewish and that the book was written primarily to a Jewish audience. This is important because later Christian writings were more and more written from the perspective of and written to non-Jewish cultures, frequently addressing pagan ideas. The fact that the book of Matthew is an appeal to Jews (chapter 10) that Jesus was their Messiah is strong indication that it was written early, when Christianity was first emerging as an offshoot of Judaism.

The writing of the book of Matthew does not appear to be a translation from Hebrew to Greek. That said, the book uses a variety of Hebrew expressions and wording that indicate that the author was from a Jewish background or had Jewish influences[21].

Moreover, the author of the book of Matthew appears to be very familiar with the geography of Israel (2:23), with the customs of Israel (1:18-19), and with the history and political climate of the time (he refers to Herod Antipas "tetrarch" instead of "king"). The author also shows a concern for Old Testament Law (5:17-20).

The author of Matthew cites the Old Testament more frequently than other Gospels, and several of his citations appear to be *his own* translation of Hebrew scripture into Greek language rather than quoting the LXX (an early Greek translation of the Hebrew Bible, c. 200 BCE)[21].

Matthew also highlights Jesus' attacks on Jewish religious leaders more than the other Gospels. A tax collector for Rome would naturally be at odds with Jewish leaders.

Matthew orders his text with numeric intent, and tends to write in a numeric fashion more than a chronological one (ordering the five great sermons of Jesus, the six corrections of law, the seven parables, etc.). Matthew's gospel focuses more heavily on money than the other gospels, containing parables and Jesus' teachings on money not contained in the other gospels. Additionally, Matthew uses monetary and tax collector terms in his writing. His version of the Lord's Prayer interprets "forgive us our debts" versus Luke's version that interprets as "forgive us our sins" or "forgive us our trespasses."

Finally, the way in which the book of Matthew talks about the disciple Matthew is unique. In the other gospels when Matthew is called by Jesus, he is referred to as "Levi." Only the book of Matthew calls him "Matthew." When the gospels list the disciples, only the book of Matthew refers to him as "Matthew, the tax collector." (Matthew 10:3)

In the book of Luke, when "Levi" is called, Luke records that he "left everything" in order to follow Jesus. The book of Matthew takes a more humble approach of saying that he "got up and followed."

To sum up:

- Many early church writers mention that Matthew wrote a gospel for the Jews
- Every single manuscript of the book of Matthew credits Matthew as the author
- The author of the book appears to be Jewish by his concern with prophecy, his familiarity with Jewish Law, customs, history, and language, and with his concern of the evangelism of the Jewish people
- The author of the book makes more intimate and humble references to Matthew, the disciple
- The author is more concerned with numerology and with money than any other Gospel writer

If Matthew was the author of this book or if this book was compiled from Matthew's testimony, then what it contains is eyewitness accounts to the life and acts of Jesus.

Chapter 8
EVIDENCE FOR THE BOOK OF *MARK*

Who was Mark?

The Bible doesn't make any overt references to Mark until the book of Acts, where he is seen accompanying Paul and Barnabas on their missionary journeys. Colossians 4:10 reveals that John Mark was actually a cousin of Barnabas, which may account for the fact that Barnabas stood up for Mark after he had abandoned Paul at one point, leading to the split between Paul and Barnabas (Acts 15:36-41).

Tradition claims that John Mark wrote the Gospel of Mark, transcribing what Peter had taught him regarding the life of Jesus[23].

Speculation on the Authorship of Mark

The Gospel of Mark is an incredibly important book. Since it is one of the few texts that practically all scholars agree was written early[24], a defense of the eyewitness accounts from this book are more likely to be taken seriously than almost any other Gospel.

In his lecture series *The Quest: The Historian's Search for Jesus and Muhammad*[17], scholar F. E. Peters nicely summarized what a significant number of historians believe. He says that the Gospels were produced decades or centuries after Jesus' life based on two sources: the *Gospel of Mark*, which they believe was written early, and contains a rudimentary outline of Jesus' deeds; and a theoretical document called "Q" that they believed was a mostly oral tradition of Jesus' teachings.

This being the case, defending the authenticity of the Gospel of Mark is slightly easier than the other three, because practically all scholars agree it was written early. This does not quite get us out of the woods. In his book *Who Wrote the Gospels*[25], critic Randel McCraw Helms makes the assertion that Mark was a Gentile document probably written by a Christian in Syria. His reasons for believing this are that (he says) the author of Mark seems unknowledgeable about Hebrew scripture (citations of Old Testament passages are a mix between the Hebrew and Greek translations, and some of the Old Testament citations mix passages from various books in the OT), and unknowledgeable about Israel's geography (Mark has Jesus travel from Jerico to Bethphage to Bethany to Jerusalem when those geographic areas are out of order).

The reason Mark is believed to be an early document even by liberal scholars is because the composition of the document is rather disjointed and the events it lists aren't well connected, which is taken as a sign that it is a primitive document.

To defend Mark, we are first going to look at the claim that Mark received his Gospel from Peter.

Was the book of Mark written from Peter's testimony?

External support

The Muratorian Fragment

A very early fragmentary document, dated around CE 170, contains a list of the gospels. Of Mark, it says:

But he was present among them, and so he put [the facts down in his Gospel[23]

While this is not much to go by, it does appear to reference someone present at the teachings of the Apostles who recorded their words

Eusebius

Eusebius was a Christian Historian who lived around 300 years after Christ. In his histories, Eusebius cites a number of earlier sources that are lost to us. One such source is Papias of Hierapolis, an early church bishop who lived about 80 years after Jesus. In his five-volume work, *Interpretation of the Oracles of the Lord* (which no longer survives), Papias wrote that the disciples of the early apostles attested that John Mark scribed his book in Rome from Peter's testimony (that goes apostles> apostle's followers> Papias> Eusebius). Eusebius quotes directly from Papias' writings:

And the elder used to say this, Mark became Peter's interpreter and wrote accurately all that he remembered, not, indeed, in order, of the things said and done by the Lord. For he had not heard the Lord, nor had followed him, but later on, followed Peter, who used to give teaching as necessity demanded but not making, as it were, an arrangement of the Lord's oracles, so that Mark did nothing wrong in thus writing down single points as he remembered them. For to one thing he gave attention, to leave out nothing of what he had heard and to make no false statements in them.[23]

Eusebius also quotes Origen (CE 185-254) as writing:

In his first book on Matthew's Gospel, maintaining the Canon of the Church, he testifies that he knows only four Gospels, writing as follows: Among the four Gospels, which are the only indisputable ones in the Church of God under heaven, I have learned by tradition that the first was written by Matthew, who was once a publican, but afterwards an apostle of Jesus Christ, and it was prepared for the converts from Judaism, and

47

published in the Hebrew language. The second is by Mark, who composed it according to the instructions of Peter, who in his Catholic epistle acknowledges him as a son, saying, "The church that is at Babylon elected together with you, salutes you, and so does Marcus, my son." [1 Peter 5:13] And the third by Luke, the Gospel commended by Paul, and composed for Gentile converts. Last of all that by John.[23]

Eusebius also quotes Clement of Alexandria (CE 150-215) as saying:

And so great a joy of light shone upon the minds of the hearers of Peter that they were not satisfied with merely a single hearing or with the unwritten teaching of the divine gospel, but with all sorts of entreaties they besought Mark, who was a follower of Peter and whose gospel is extant, to leave behind with them in writing a record of the teaching passed on to them orally; and they did not cease until they had prevailed upon the man and so became responsible for the Scripture for reading in the churches.[23]

Eusebius writes a similar passage with a few differences that indicates he may have had a third source to go on:

Again, in the same books, Clement gives the tradition of the earliest presbyters, as to the order of the Gospels, in the following manner: The Gospels containing the genealogies, he says, were written first. The Gospel according to Mark had this occasion. As Peter had preached the Word publicly at Rome, and declared the Gospel by the Spirit, many who were present requested that Mark, who had followed him for a long time and remembered his sayings, should write them out. And having composed the Gospel he gave it to those who had requested it. When Peter learned of this, he neither directly forbade nor encouraged it.[26]

The interesting thing here is the detail about Peter not knowing until after the gospel had been written. Since this is a unique detail not found in other sources, it indicates that Eusebius may have had another source to go on.

Irenaus

Irenaus, a Christian Apologist who lived about 150 years after Jesus, wrote:

> Matthew composed his gospel among the Hebrews in their own language, while Peter and Paul proclaimed the gospel in Rome and founded the community. After their departure, Mark, the disciple and interpreter of Peter, handed on his preaching to us in written form[23].

Justin Martyr

Justin Martyr, also a Christian Apologist who lived around 150 years after Jesus, wrote that Peter's memoirs record Jesus renaming the sons of Zebedee "Sons of Thunder." This reference is only found in the book of Mark, a strong indication that Mark contains the "memoirs" to which Justin refers[23].

Tertullian

Tertullian was a prolific Christian writer from North Africa and lived about 200 years after Jesus. In his book, *Against Marcion*, Tertullian writes:

> While that [gospel] which Mark published may be affirmed to be Peter's whose interpreter Mark was.[23]

Anti-Marcionite Prologue

In some early collections of scripture that date from around 300 years after Jesus, there are a series of prologues to the gospels. The prologue to Mark reads:

> Mark declared, who is called "stump-fingered," because he had rather small fingers in comparison with the stature of the rest of his body. He was the interpreter of Peter. After the death of Peter himself he wrote down this same gospel in the regions of Italy.[23]

Look for differences

The important thing to look for when comparing these early testimonies is the difference in details. If all of them are just parroting some previous rumor, they are all going to sound similar. The fact that Eusebius is citing four separate, unique sources in his history, the offhanded comment that Justin Martyr makes to the "sons of thunder" and the unique personal detail contained in the Anti-Marcionite Prologue are all examples of original accounts. These lend credibility to the claim that Mark transcribed for Peter.

Why name a Gospel after Mark?

John Mark is a very minor figure in the New Testament. Of the various people who could be attributed for the writing of a Gospel if one were being deceitful, Mark would be very far down the list. The fact that the Gospel is attributed to such a minor character is actually evidence that Mark had a hand in writing it.

Mark's relationship with Peter

There is also Biblical support for the idea that Mark and Peter had a close relationship. The book of Acts describes Peter's miraculous escape from prison. In that account, we see that Peter attended a congregation of believers that actually met in John Mark's house:

> **Acts 12:12-14**
> English Standard Version (ESV)
>
> [12] When he realized this, he went to the house of Mary, the mother of John whose other name was Mark, where many were gathered together and were praying. [13] And when he knocked at the door of the gateway, a servant girl named Rhoda came to answer. [14] Recognizing Peter's voice, in her

joy she did not open the gate but ran in and reported that Peter was standing at the gate.

In his first epistle, Peter describes his relationship with Mark as that of a father and son:

1 Peter 5:13
English Standard Version (ESV)

[13] She who is at Babylon, who is likewise chosen, sends you greetings, and so does Mark, my son.

Since these two passages by two different authors mention Mark in close connection with Peter, it is reasonable to assume that the two had some kind of acquaintance. This makes the claim that Mark wrote for Peter seem more reasonable.

Internal Support

Writing Style

The book of *Mark*, like all of the other gospels, is written in Greek. However the author of *Mark* does not appear to use Greek fluidly. He appears by the writing style to be penning the book in a second language. How can this be told? Mostly by literary style and syntax. Consider the difference between English and Spanish. In English, the narrator will list the adjectives describing a noun, then place the noun at the end. They might say something like "the big, round, red ball." In Spanish, the speaker gives the noun, then lists the adjectives to describe it. So the same sentence would look like this: "the ball, big, round, red."

The author of *Mark* constructs his sentences in a way that is more common to Aramaic syntax than it is to Greek syntax. Since John Mark was a Palestinian Jew, and Palestinian Jews would have spoken Aramaic as a first language, the writing style supports the idea that John Mark may have been the author.

Outline

The book of Acts gives several samples of Peter's preaching style:

Acts 1:21-22
English Standard Version (ESV)

[21] So one of the men who have accompanied us during all the time that the Lord Jesus went in and out among us, [22] beginning from the baptism of John until the day when he was taken up from us—one of these men must become with us a witness to his resurrection."

Acts 10:37-41
English Standard Version (ESV)

[37] you yourselves know what happened throughout all Judea, beginning from Galilee after the baptism that John proclaimed: [38] how God anointed Jesus of Nazareth with the Holy Spirit and with power. He went about doing good and healing all who were oppressed by the devil, for God was with him. [39] And we are witnesses of all that he did both in the country of the Jews and in Jerusalem. They put him to death by hanging him on a tree, [40] but God raised him on the third day and made him to appear, [41] not to all the people but to us who had been chosen by God as witnesses, who ate and drank with him after he rose from the dead.

As seen by these two passages, Peter's summary of the life of Christ begins with his baptism by John, his public ministry and miracles, his death, his resurrection, and his ascension. This is exactly how the book of Mark flows.

What Mark does not include is the birth narrative of Jesus, and some of the more private information about Jesus' family found in the other gospels.

How the Gospel treats the person of Peter

If studied alongside the other Gospels, it is interesting to note that *Mark* leaves out a number of details that the others include relating to Peter. For instance, there are a good number of rash and embarrassing things that Peter did that are not mentioned in *Mark*. These are as follows:

Miraculous Catch

Peter, Andrew, James, and John were all called to the ministry by Jesus at one time. They were all partners in the fishing industry. The book of Luke records their calling like this:

Luke 5:1-11
English Standard Version (ESV)

Jesus Calls the First Disciples

5 On one occasion, while the crowd was pressing in on him to hear the word of God, he was standing by the lake of Gennesaret, ² and he saw two boats by the lake, but the fishermen had gone out of them and were washing their nets. ³ Getting into one of the boats, which was Simon's, he asked him to put out a little from the land. And he sat down and taught the people from the boat. ⁴ And when he had finished speaking, he said to Simon, "Put out into the deep and let down your nets for a catch." ⁵ And Simon answered, "Master, we toiled all night and took nothing! But at your word I will let down the nets." ⁶ And when they had done this, they enclosed a large number of fish, and their nets were breaking. ⁷ They signaled to their partners in the other boat to come and help them. And they came and filled both the boats, so that they began to sink. ⁸ But when Simon Peter saw it, he fell down at Jesus' knees, saying, "Depart from me, for I am a sinful man, O Lord." ⁹ For he and all who were with him were astonished at the catch of fish that they had taken, ¹⁰ and so also were James and John, sons of Zebedee, who were partners with Simon. And Jesus said to Simon, "Do not be afraid; from now on you will be catching men." ¹¹ And when they had brought their boats to land, they left everything and followed him.

Notice that in this account, Peter is the first to doubt Jesus, and his reaction to the miracle is extreme compared to the others: falling on his face and confessing his sinfulness.

This is how *Mark* describes the same incident:

Mark 1:16-20
English Standard Version (ESV)

Jesus Calls the First Disciples

¹⁶ Passing alongside the Sea of Galilee, he saw Simon and Andrew the brother of Simon casting a net into the sea, for they were fishermen. ¹⁷ And Jesus said to them, "Follow me, and I will make you become fishers of men." ¹⁸ And immediately they left their nets and followed him. ¹⁹ And going on a little farther, he saw James the son of Zebedee and John his brother, who were in their boat mending the

nets. [20] And immediately he called them, and they left their father Zebedee in the boat with the hired servants and followed him.

Notice that in this instance, it is a brief summary of the same event. It mentions Peter (Simon) first in the order of those called, but omits the details that would have rendered him in a less than flattering light.

The Woman with the issue of blood

In a passage in *Mark*, the book describes the healing of a woman with an issue of blood:

Mark 5:21-34
English Standard Version (ESV)

[21] And when Jesus had crossed again in the boat to the other side, a great crowd gathered about him, and he was beside the sea. [22] Then came one of the rulers of the synagogue, Jairus by name, and seeing him, he fell at his feet [23] and implored him earnestly, saying, "My little daughter is at the point of death. Come and lay your hands on her, so that she may be made well and live." [24] And he went with him.

And a great crowd followed him and thronged about him. [25] And there was a woman who had had a discharge of blood for twelve years, [26] and who had suffered much under many physicians, and had spent all that she had, and was no better but rather grew worse. [27] She had heard the reports about Jesus and came up behind him in the crowd and touched his garment. [28] For she said, "If I touch even his garments, I will be made well." [29] And immediately the flow of blood dried up, and she felt in her body that she was healed of her disease. [30] And Jesus, perceiving in himself that power had gone out from him, immediately turned about in the crowd and said, "Who touched my garments?" [31] And his disciples said to him, "You see the crowd pressing around you, and yet you say, 'Who touched me?'" [32] And he looked around to see who had done it. [33] But the woman, knowing what had happened to her, came in fear and trembling and fell down before him and told him the whole truth. [34] And he said to her, "Daughter, your faith has made you well; go in peace, and be healed of your disease."

Pay particular attention to verse 31 where it says "And his disciples said to him, "You see the crowd pressing around you, and yet you say, 'Who touched me?'"

This somewhat sarcastic and disrespectful comment is attributed generally to "his disciples." Now notice how the book of Luke renders the same account:

Luke 8:42-48
English Standard Version (ESV)

[42] for he had an only daughter, about twelve years of age, and she was dying.

As Jesus went, the people pressed around him. [43] And there was a woman who had had a discharge of blood for twelve years, and though she had spent all her living on physicians, she could not be healed by anyone. [44] She came up behind him and touched the fringe of his garment, and immediately her discharge of blood ceased. [45] And Jesus said, "Who was it that touched me?" When all denied it, Peter said, "Master, the crowds surround you and are pressing in on you!" ⁴⁶ But Jesus said, "Someone touched me, for I perceive that power has gone out from me." ⁴⁷ And when the woman saw that she was not hidden, she came trembling, and falling down before him declared in the presence of all the people why she had touched him, and how she had been immediately healed. ⁴⁸ And he said to her, "Daughter, your faith has made you well; go in peace."

Notice in verse 45, it is specifically Peter who makes this statement. Once again, *Mark* appears to be protecting Peter from embarrassment.

Parable of defilement

The book of Matthew records a parable of Jesus and Peter's response to the miracle:

Matthew 15:10-18
English Standard Version (ESV)

¹⁰ And he called the people to him and said to them, "Hear and understand: ¹¹ it is not what goes into the mouth that defiles a person, but what comes out of the mouth; this defiles a person." ¹² Then the disciples came and said to him, "Do you know that the Pharisees were offended when they heard this saying?" ¹³ He answered, "Every plant that my heavenly Father has not planted will be rooted up. ¹⁴ Let them alone; they are blind guides. And if the blind lead the blind, both will fall into a pit." ¹⁵ But Peter said to him, "Explain the parable to us." ¹⁶ And he said, "Are you also still without understanding? ¹⁷ Do you not see that whatever

goes into the mouth passes into the stomach and is expelled?[18] But what comes out of the mouth proceeds from the heart, and this defiles a person.

As per usual, Peter is the first to speak up and ask for an explanation to the parable, and Jesus takes him to task for his lack of understanding. The book of Mark records the same event like this:

Mark 7:14-19
English Standard Version (ESV)

What Defiles a Person

[14] And he called the people to him again and said to them, "Hear me, all of you, and understand: [15] There is nothing outside a person that by going into him can defile him, but the things that come out of a person are what defile him." [17] And when he had entered the house and left the people, his disciples asked him about the parable. [18] And he said to them, "Then are you also without understanding? Do you not see that whatever goes into a person from outside cannot defile him, [19] since it enters not his heart but his stomach, and is expelled?" (Thus he declared all foods clean.)

The first thing to notice is that, as we would expect by this point, Peter's embarrassing question and Jesus' rebuke are generally attributed to "his disciples." Once again, Mark is protecting Peter.

Perhaps more interestingly, though, is the end of the passage where *Mark* adds the parenthetical note "Thus he declared all foods clean." This is telling because of an experience Peter has in the book of Acts:

Acts 10:9-16
English Standard Version (ESV)

[9] The next day, as they were on their journey and approaching the city, Peter went up on the housetop about the sixth hour to pray. [10] And he became hungry and wanted something to eat, but while they were preparing it, he fell into a trance [11] and saw the heavens opened and something like a great sheet descending, being let down by its four corners upon the earth. [12] In it were all kinds of animals and reptiles and birds of the air. [13] And there came a voice to him: "Rise, Peter; kill and eat." [14] But Peter said, "By no means, Lord; for I have never eaten anything that is common or unclean." [15] And the voice came to him again a second time, "What God has made clean, do not call common." [16] This happened three times, and the thing was taken up at once to heaven.

This particular vision was God's way of telling Peter that He wanted the Gospel preached to all men, not simply circumcised Jews. But the incidental of this account was that God appears to be redacting the dietary laws of Moses. Since this was an experience peculiar to Peter, it appears to be reflected in this account in the book of *Mark*.

Walking on the water

Both *Matthew* and *Mark* contain an account of Jesus walking on the water. *Matthew's* account goes like this:

Matthew 14:22-33
English Standard Version (ESV)

[22] Immediately he made the disciples get into the boat and go before him to the other side, while he dismissed the crowds. [23] And after he had dismissed the crowds, he went up on the mountain by himself to pray. When evening came, he was there alone, [24] but the boat by this time was a long way from the land, beaten by the waves, for the wind was against them. [25] And in the fourth watch of the night he came to them, walking on the sea. [26] But when the disciples saw him walking on the sea, they were terrified, and said, "It is a ghost!" and they cried out in fear. [27] But immediately Jesus spoke to them, saying, "Take heart; it is I. Do not be afraid."

[28] And Peter answered him, "Lord, if it is you, command me to come to you on the water." [29] He said, "Come." So Peter got out of the boat and walked on the water and came to Jesus. [30] But when he saw the wind, he was afraid, and beginning to sink he cried out, "Lord, save me." [31] Jesus immediately reached out his hand and took hold of him, saying to him, "O you of little faith, why did you doubt?" [32] And when they got into the boat, the wind ceased. [33] And those in the boat worshiped him, saying, "Truly you are the Son of God."

This is possibly the most familiar account of Peter's impulsiveness followed by a lack of faith. *Mark*, of course, completely omits that bit:

Mark 6:45-51
English Standard Version (ESV)

45 Immediately he made his disciples get into the boat and go before him to the other side, to Bethsaida, while he dismissed the crowd. 46 And after he had taken leave of them, he went up on the mountain to pray. 47 And when evening came, the boat was out on the sea, and he was alone on the land. 48 And he saw that they were making headway painfully, for the wind was against them. And about the fourth watch of the night he came to them, walking on the sea. He meant to pass by them, 49 but when they saw him walking on the sea they thought it was a ghost, and cried out, 50 for they all saw him and were terrified. But immediately he spoke to them and said, "Take heart; it is I. Do not be afraid." 51 And he got into the boat with them, and the wind ceased. And they were utterly astounded.

Jesus rebukes Peter

The book of Matthew records a particularly harsh rebuke that Jesus levels at Peter:

Matthew 16:21-23
English Standard Version (ESV)

Jesus Foretells His Death and Resurrection

21 From that time Jesus began to show his disciples that he must go to Jerusalem and suffer many things from the elders and chief priests and scribes, and be killed, and on the third day be raised. 22 And Peter took him aside and began to rebuke him, saying, "Far be it from you, Lord! This shall never happen to

61

you." [23] But he turned and said to Peter, "Get behind me, Satan! You are a hindrance to me. For you are not setting your mind on the things of God, but on the things of man."

While Mark records the same event with the same rebuke, there are slight differences:

Mark 8:31-33
English Standard Version (ESV)

Jesus Foretells His Death and Resurrection

[31] And he began to teach them that the Son of Man must suffer many things and be rejected by the elders and the chief priests and the scribes and be killed, and after three days rise again. [32] And he said this plainly. And Peter took him aside and began to rebuke him. [33] But turning and seeing his disciples, he rebuked Peter and said, "Get behind me, Satan! For you are not setting your mind on the things of God, but on the things of man."

Notice that Mark stresses that this conversation occurred in private, and that Jesus was mindful of the other disciples when rebuking Peter. Secondly, Mark leaves out Peter's specific words when Peter rebuked Jesus. This is an embarrassment to Peter no matter how you cut it, but Mark tries to soften the blow.

Leaving all to follow Jesus

After Jesus sent away the rich young ruler, he turned to his disciples and said:

Matthew 19:23-30
English Standard Version (ESV)

[23] And Jesus said to his disciples, "Truly, I say to you, only with difficulty will a rich person enter the kingdom of heaven. [24] Again I tell you, it is easier for a camel to go through the eye of a needle than for a rich person to enter the kingdom of God." [25] When the disciples heard this, they were greatly astonished, saying, "Who then can be saved?" [26] But Jesus looked at them and said, "With man this is impossible, but with God all things are possible." [27] Then Peter said in reply, "See, we have left everything and followed you. What then will we have?" [28] Jesus said to them, "Truly, I say to you, in the new world, when the Son of Man will sit on his glorious throne, you who have followed me will also sit on twelve thrones, judging the twelve tribes of Israel. [29] And everyone who has left houses or brothers or sisters or father or mother or children or lands, for my name's sake, will receive a hundredfold and will inherit eternal life. [30] But many who are first will be last, and the last first.

This is how *Mark* renders the same account:

Mark 10:23-31
English Standard Version (ESV)

[23] And Jesus looked around and said to his disciples, "How difficult it will be for those who have wealth to enter the kingdom of God!" [24] And the disciples were amazed at his words. But Jesus said to them again, "Children, how difficult it is to enter the kingdom of God! [25] It is easier for a camel to go through the eye of a needle than for a rich

person to enter the kingdom of God." [26] And they were exceedingly astonished, and said to him, "Then who can be saved?" [27] Jesus looked at them and said, "With man it is impossible, but not with God. For all things are possible with God." [28] Peter began to say to him, "See, we have left everything and followed you." [29] Jesus said, "Truly, I say to you, there is no one who has left house or brothers or sisters or mother or father or children or lands, for my sake and for the gospel, [30] who will not receive a hundredfold now in this time, houses and brothers and sisters and mothers and children and lands, with persecutions, and in the age to come eternal life. [31] But many who are first will be last, and the last first."

While both *Matthew* and *Mark* have Peter speaking up about how they have left everything for the sake of Jesus, *Matthew* has Peter follow up by saying "What then will we have?" Not only is Peter self-congratulating in this passage, he's also being a bit greedy looking for some reward for their sacrifice. *Mark* omits this selfish question.

Jesus predicts Peter's denial

Possibly the worst action ever recorded of Peter was his denial of Jesus. At the Passover celebration before Jesus was arrested, Jesus predicted Peter's denial. None of the accounts are particularly flattering to Peter. Luke's account goes this way:

Luke 22:31-34
English Standard Version (ESV)

Jesus Foretells Peter's Denial

[31] "Simon, Simon, behold, Satan demanded to have you, that he might sift you like wheat,[32] but I have

prayed for you that your faith may not fail. And when you have turned again, strengthen your brothers." [33] Peter said to him, "Lord, I am ready to go with you both to prison and to death." [34] Jesus said, "I tell you, Peter, the rooster will not crow this day, until you deny three times that you know me."

In this account, Peter is singled out as being a particular target of Satan.

This is *John's* account of the same incident:

John 13:34-38
English Standard Version (ESV)

[34] A new commandment I give to you, that you love one another: just as I have loved you, you also are to love one another. [35] By this all people will know that you are my disciples, if you have love for one another."

Jesus Foretells Peter's Denial

[36] Simon Peter said to him, "Lord, where are you going?" Jesus answered him, "Where I am going you cannot follow me now, but you will follow afterward." [37] Peter said to him, "Lord, why can I not follow you now? I will lay down my life for you." [38] Jesus answered, "Will you lay down your life for me? Truly, truly, I say to you, the rooster will not crow till you have denied me three times.

In this passage, Peter is seen asking some pretty naïve questions regarding "Where are you going?"

Finally, Mark's account:

Mark 14:27-31
English Standard Version (ESV)

[27] And Jesus said to them, "You will all fall away, for it is written, 'I will strike the shepherd, and the sheep will be scattered.' [28] But after I am raised up, I will go before you to Galilee." [29] Peter said to him, "Even though they all fall away, I will not." [30] And Jesus said to him, "Truly, I tell you, this very night, before the rooster crows twice, you will deny me three times." [31] But he said emphatically, "If I must die with you, I will not deny you." And they all said the same.

Mark also records Jesus' prediction of Peter's denial and Peter's response. But it is interesting to note that Mark omits both Peter's naïve questions, and Jesus' reference to Satan's work in Peter's life. Most importantly, Mark has the disciples chiming in with Peter's bold claim to follow Jesus to the death. Mark has all the disciples sharing Peter's embarrassment so as not to single Peter out.

The foot-washing

The book of John records an incident that occurred at the Last Supper in which Jesus humbly washes the feet of his disciples. As always, Peter has something rash and impulsive to say during this event:

John 13:2-9
English Standard Version (ESV)

[2] During supper, when the devil had already put it into the heart of Judas Iscariot, Simon's son, to betray him, [3] Jesus, knowing that the Father had

given all things into his hands, and that he had come from God and was going back to God, ⁴ rose from supper. He laid aside his outer garments, and taking a towel, tied it around his waist. ⁵ Then he poured water into a basin and began to wash the disciples' feet and to wipe them with the towel that was wrapped around him. ⁶ He came to Simon Peter, who said to him, "Lord, do you wash my feet?" ⁷ Jesus answered him, "What I am doing you do not understand now, but afterward you will understand." ⁸ Peter said to him, "You shall never wash my feet." Jesus answered him, "If I do not wash you, you have no share with me." ⁹ Simon Peter said to him, "Lord, not my feet only but also my hands and my head!"

The Gospel of Mark entirely omits this event.

Peter's denial of Jesus

It is now time to examine the single most shameful event in Peter's life: his denial of Christ. This is how Luke's Gospel tells the event:

Luke 22:54-62
English Standard Version (ESV)

Peter Denies Jesus

⁵⁴ Then they seized him and led him away, bringing him into the high priest's house, and Peter was following at a distance. ⁵⁵ And when they had kindled a fire in the middle of the courtyard and sat down together, Peter sat down among them. ⁵⁶ Then a servant girl, seeing him as he sat in the light and looking closely

at him, said, "This man also was with him."[57] But he denied it, saying, "Woman, I do not know him." [58] And a little later someone else saw him and said, "You also are one of them." But Peter said, "Man, I am not." [59] And after an interval of about an hour still another insisted, saying, "Certainly this man also was with him, for he too is a Galilean." [60] But Peter said, "Man, I do not know what you are talking about." And immediately, while he was still speaking, the rooster crowed. [61] And the Lord turned and looked at Peter. And Peter remembered the saying of the Lord, how he had said to him, "Before the rooster crows today, you will deny me three times." [62] And he went out and wept bitterly.

Luke certainly doesn't pull any punches in this account. Peter's denials are each direct quotations, they are blunt denials of his relationship with Jesus, and after the denials, Jesus turns and looks directly at Peter.

Here is Mark's account:

Mark 14:66-72
English Standard Version (ESV)

Peter Denies Jesus

And as Peter was below in the courtyard, one of the servant girls of the high priest came,[67] and seeing Peter warming himself, she looked at him and said, "You also were with the Nazarene, Jesus." [68] But he denied it, saying, "I neither know nor understand what you mean." And he went out into the gateway and the rooster crowed. [69] And the servant girl saw him and began again to say to the bystanders, "This man is one of them." [70] But again he denied it. And after a little while the bystanders again said to Peter, "Certainly you are one of them, for you are a Galilean." [71] But he began to invoke a curse on himself and to swear, "I do not know this man of whom you speak." [72] And immediately the rooster crowed a second time. And Peter remembered how Jesus had said to him, "Before the rooster crows twice, you will deny me three times." And he broke down and wept.

In this account Peter's first denial is a claim that he doesn't understand what she is saying. He doesn't directly deny his relationship with Jesus yet, just says he can't understand her. When accused a second time, *Mark* just says "But he again denied it." Finally, on the third denial, *Mark* has Peter calling down curses *on himself*. He apparently is already feeling the shame of what he is doing. He doesn't curse Jesus or the accusers, but directs his anger at himself. Then Mark omits the direct look that Jesus gives Peter before he breaks down weeping.

Simon receives his new name "Peter"

In the book of *Matthew*, the author writes this:

Matthew 16:13-20
English Standard Version (ESV)

Peter Confesses Jesus as the Christ

[13] Now when Jesus came into the district of Caesarea Philippi, he asked his disciples, "Who do people say that the Son of Man is?" [14] And they said, "Some say John the Baptist, others say Elijah, and others Jeremiah or one of the prophets." [15] He said to them, "But who do you say that I am?" [16] Simon Peter replied, "You are the Christ, the Son of the living God."[17] And Jesus

answered him, "Blessed are you, Simon Bar-Jonah! For flesh and blood has not revealed this to you, but my Father who is in heaven. [18] And I tell you, you are Peter, and on this rock I will build my church, and the gates of hell shall not prevail against it. [19] I will give you the keys of the kingdom of heaven, and whatever you bind on earth shall be bound in heaven, and whatever you loose on earth shall be loosed in heaven." [20] Then he strictly charged the disciples to tell no one that he was the Christ.

In this instance, Peter is actually complimented for his confession of Jesus as Messiah. Mark records it like this:

Mark 8:27-30
English Standard Version (ESV)

Peter Confesses Jesus as the Christ

[27] And Jesus went on with his disciples to the villages of Caesarea Philippi. And on the way he asked his disciples, "Who do people say that I am?" [28] And they told him, "John the Baptist; and others say, Elijah; and others, one of the prophets." [29] And he asked them, "But who do you say that I am?" Peter answered him, "You are the Christ." [30] And he strictly charged them to tell no one about him.

This passage oddly leaves out Jesus' compliment to Peter for his confession. If Mark was writing this narration from Peter's teaching, Peter may have omitted this detail out of modesty.

The above listed omissions and delicate wordings are not all of the examples available, simply some of the more obvious ones. The ways in which these are worded seem to indicate that the author had a personal investment in protecting Peter and casting him in the best light possible.

Accounts that are unique to Mark's Gospel

It is not simply the things that were omitted from *Mark's* account that are important, but also the things included. *Mark* includes a number of details that are unique to Peter's perspective. Most of them are incidental, not important to the point of the story, which makes them all the more telling of Peter's influence on the text.

Take, for instance, this account from the first chapter of Mark:

Mark 1:35-37
English Standard Version (ESV)

Jesus Preaches in Galilee

[35] And rising very early in the morning, while it was still dark, he departed and went out to a desolate place, and there he prayed. [36] And Simon and those who were with him searched for him, [37] and they found him and said to him, "Everyone is looking for you."

Note that Simon Peter is the primary focus, and the other disciples are written very incidentally as "those who were with him." If the story had been written from, say, Phillip's point of view, it might have said "Phillips and those who were with him searched for Jesus." There is no reason to list Peter as the main player unless the story is being told by Peter.

The Mention of Capernaum

The book of *Matthew* (4:13-16) mentions that after the execution of John the Baptist, Jesus changed residence from

Nazareth to Capernaum, possibly to avoid being arrested in connection with John.

The first chapter of *Mark* gives us the additional detail that Peter's mother-in-law lived in Capernaum, which may indicate that Jesus' residence was in Peter's house in Capernaum. The healing of Peter's mother-in-law is recorded only in the book of *Mark*, and this is the only book from which we get the detail of Peter's residence in Capernaum

There is an event that occurs in Capernaum wherein Jesus heals a paralyzed man. While both *Matthew* and *Mark* record this miracle (*Luke* then copies the miracle from *Mark's* account), Mark's description is much more explicit. Compare:

Matthew 9:1-2
English Standard Version (ESV)

Jesus Heals a Paralytic

9 And getting into a boat he crossed over and came to his own city. ² And behold, some people brought to him a paralytic, lying on a bed. And when Jesus saw their faith, he said to the paralytic, "Take heart, my son; your sins are forgiven."

And *Mark's* account:

Mark 2:1-5
English Standard Version (ESV)

Jesus Heals a Paralytic

2 And when he returned to Capernaum after some days, it was reported that he was at home. ² And many were gathered together, so that there was no more room, not even at the door. And he was preaching the word to them. [3] And they came, bringing to him a paralytic carried by four men. [4] And when they could not get near him because of the crowd, they removed the roof above him, and when they had made an opening, they let down the bed on which the paralytic lay. [5] And when Jesus saw their faith, he said to the paralytic, "Son, your sins are forgiven."

Notice that *Mark* says that it was reported that "he was home," and then the crowds gathered, presumably at his house. Since the house he was in was probably Peter's house or that of Peter's mother-in-law, it makes sense that *Mark* records the roof being ripped up from the house. After all, that was *his roof* that was being removed.

The Fig Tree

Matthew records the cursing of the fig tree like this:

Matthew 21:18-19
English Standard Version (ESV)

Jesus Curses the Fig Tree

[18] In the morning, as he was returning to the city, he became hungry. [19] And seeing a fig tree by the wayside, he went to it and found nothing on it but only leaves. And he said to it, "May no fruit ever come from you again!" And the fig tree withered at once.

And *Mark* says it this way:

Mark 11:20-21
English Standard Version (ESV)

The Lesson from the Withered Fig Tree

[20] As they passed by in the morning, they saw the fig tree withered away to its roots.[21] And Peter remembered and said to him, "Rabbi, look! The fig tree that you cursed has withered."

Note that Mark's gospel identifies Peter as the disciple who noticed the fig tree had withered. This detail is not in any way important to the story, but it once again places Peter as the main character in the story.

Other Evidences for *Mark*

The concept that John Mark wrote the book based on the teachings of Peter is not the only evidence for the validity of this Gospel. Here we will look at other evidences for the early dating and eyewitness nature of the book.

Archeological Evidence

In 1947, documents were discovered hidden in clay pots in a series of caves along the northwest bank of the Dead Sea. These scrolls dated from as early as 150 BCE to as late as CE 70. While most of the scrolls were Hebrew Language documents, including many from the Old Testament, one cave contained Greek Language documents.

In 1972, a papyrologist named Jose O'Callaghan was examining some of the scrolls when he discovered a fragment that contained this text in Greek:

*"For they did not understand concerning the loaves
but was their heart hardened. And crossing over [unto
the land] they came unto Gennesaret and drew to the
shore. And coming forth out of the boat immediately
they recognized him.*[27]*"*

He identified this passage as Mark 6:52-53. The type of
Greek Script in which the fragment is written is consistent with
a style that was used up until CE 50. The documents stashed in
the caves date as late as CE 68, making this fragment of Mark date
fairly early.

Since O'Callaghan made this discovery, his findings were
confirmed by a number of other eminent scholars.

However, nothing is ever that simple with ancient
documents. These are handwritten texts on papyrus scrolls that are
badly faded, and will be missing pieces that make reconstructing
the text a challenge. Consequently, there are many scholars
who have attacked O'Callaghan's conclusion by arguing that he
misinterpreted the paragraph breaks or that the word structure
makes his finding inconclusive.

While this is not the magic bullet one would hope for, it is
yet another piece of evidence added to the cumulative case that
Mark's Gospel was written early enough for him to have access to
the eyewitnesses.

The structure of Mark

In his book *Cold Case Christianity* (2013), Homicide
Detective Jim Wallace writes this:

Although Mark's gospel contains the important details
of Jesus's life and ministry, it is brief, less ordered
than the other gospels, and filled with "action" verbs
and adjectives. There is a sense of urgency about
it. This is what we might expect if it was, in fact, an

early account of Jesus' ministry, written with a sense of urgency. It is clear that the eyewitnesses felt this urgency and believed that Jesus would return very soon. Paul wrote that "salvation is nearer to us than when we believed" (Rom. 13:11), and James said, "The coming of the Lord is near" (James 5:8). Peter, Mark's mentor and companion, agreed that "the end of all things is near" (1 Pet. 4:7). Surely, Mark wrote with the same sense of urgency as he penned Peter's experiences in his own gospel[28].

Accurate Geography

Near the beginning of this section, we mentioned that critics leap at the fact that the author of *Mark* got several of his towns out of order in the travels of Jesus. However, if one were to look at a topological map of the area Jesus was traveling, they would see that the direct route goes over a fairly large mountain. The route Jesus took is the logical way to travel around the mountain through areas where he could refresh his water and supplies.

This answer is further supported by the fact that the overall geography as recorded in *Mark* is very accurate to Judea, indicating that the author or his source knew the area well. In addition to this, the history conveyed in *Mark* is accurate to the first century[29].

Conclusion

In this chapter, we have looked at the evidence that the book of *Mark* is based on eyewitness accounts. We have examined early Christian writings showing *Mark* was written based on the testimony of Peter, including the writings of:

- The Muratorian Fragment
- Eusebius

- Irenaus
- Justin Martyr
- Tertullian
- The Anti-Marcionite Prologue

We have shown from the book of *Acts* and *1 Peter* that John Mark had a close relationship with Peter, and that it would be odd to name a book after such a minor New Testament character unless he actually wrote the book.

We have shown that the writing style of the book of *Mark* is consistent with the idea that John Mark is the writer. And that the outline of *Mark* is consistent with the outline of Jesus' life that Peter gives in his sermons in *Acts*.

We have shown that the book of *Mark* tends to downplay the embarrassing episodes in Peter's life when compared to the other gospels, and that Peter is frequently the viewpoint character in Mark's gospel.

Even if the argument that John Mark wrote the book based on Peter's testimony fails, the fragment of Mark's gospel found in the Dead Sea Scrolls combined with the hurried and unstructured writing style is strong evidence that the book was written early.

Finally, the historic events, people, and geography that Mark references are accurate to the time and place in which the book is supposed to have been written.

The defense of *Mark* is important, since most scholars will allow that *Mark* is the earliest and therefore most accurate gospel.

Chapter 9
EVIDENCE FOR THE BOOK OF *LUKE*

Does the New Testament read like History or Mythology?

In his lecture series "Reliability of the Gospels[29]" Tim McGrew, professor of philosophy at Western Michigan University, makes the argument that historians maintain a double standard when reading New Testament documents as compared to other historical texts of the same time period. Thus, whereas a scholar would take the writings of Josephus at face value, they would tend to immediately dismiss any historical statements made by the book of *Acts*.

There are two principal reasons why historians categorically dismiss the New Testament documents. The first is that they are considered to be religious documents *instead of* historical documents. One might argue that this is a false dichotomy, but this leads to the second objection: they contain records of supernatural events and therefore cannot be taken seriously. One would not, for instance, take Homer's *Odyssey* with its superhumans, monsters, and squabbling gods to be a book of history, nor would one take *Journey to the West* with its dragons and talking monkeys as a serious historical record. Why take a book about magical healings and resurrection to be real history?

Of course, this displays an immediate bias against the supernatural. The entire point of the New Testament documents is to give eyewitness testimony of events that were exceptional, the claim being that these uncommon supernatural occurrences are proofs that Jesus was, indeed, the son of God. If one dismisses the testimonies that purport to be evidence for the supernatural, because they *contain* the supernatural, they have ignored the entire point of the text. Is the evidence sound or unsound?

If it really happened, then it happened in real history, and the documents that bear witness to it will bear all the hallmarks of eyewitness testimony that takes place in a real historical context.

When one compares the New Testament documents to religious and mythological texts, and then compares them with historical documents, they clearly bear more resemblance to the latter.

Take, as an example the following passages from the Bible:

The first is a passage from one of the gospels:

"In those days a decree went out from Caesar Augustus that all the world should be registered. This was the first registration when Quirinius was governor of Syria. And all went to be registered, each to his own town. And Joseph also went up from Galilee, from the town of Nazareth, to Judea, to the city of David, which is called Bethlehem, because he was of the house and lineage of David, to be registered with Mary, his betrothed, who was with child. And while they were there, the time came for her to give birth. And she gave birth to her firstborn son and wrapped him in swaddling clothes and laid him in a manger, because there was no place for them in the inn." (Luke 2:1-7 ESV)

The second is a passage from the historical book of Acts:

"Now those who were scattered because of the persecution that arose over Stephen traveled as far as Phoenicia and Cyprus and Antioch, speaking the word to no one except Jews. But there were some of them, men of Cyprus and Cyrene, who on coming to Antioch spoke to the Hellenists also, preaching the Lord Jesus. And the hand of the Lord was with them, and a great number who believed turned to the Lord. The report of this came to the ears of the church in Jerusalem, and they sent Barnabas to Antioch. When he came and saw the grace of God, he was glad, and he exhorted them all to remain faithful to the Lord with steadfast purpose, for he was a good man, full of the Holy Spirit and of faith. And a great many people were added to the Lord. So Barnabas went to Tarsus to look for Saul, and when he had found him, he brought him to Antioch. For a whole year they met with the church and taught a great many people. And in Antioch the disciples were first called Christians." (Acts 11:19-26 ESV)

The third is a passage from one of the epistles:

"I will visit you after passing through Macedonia, for I intend to pass through Macedonia, and perhaps I will stay with you or even spend the winter, so that you may help me on my journey, wherever I go. For I do not want to see you now just in passing. I hope to spend some time with you, if the Lord permits. But I will stay in Ephesus until Pentecost, for a wide door for effective work has opened to me, and there are many adversaries.

"When Timothy comes, see that you put him at ease among you, for he is doing the work of the Lord, as I am. So let no one despise him. Help him on his way in peace that he may return to me, for I am expecting him with the brothers.

"Now concerning our brother Apollos, I strongly urged him to visit you with the other brothers, but it was not at all his will to come now. He will come when he has opportunity." (1 Corinthians 16:5-12 ESV)

Excepting the apocalyptic book of Revelation, these three represent the three types of books contained in the New Testament. As seen here, while all of these books contain theological content, they couch this content in a history of supposedly real persons, places, and events.

Non-Biblical Religious text

Now compare these passages to a passage from an apocryphal book, *The Shepherd of Hermas,* which was considered and eventually rejected for inclusion in the New Testament canon:

"The master, who reared me, had sold me to one Rhoda in Rome. After many years, I met her again, and began to love her as a sister. After a certain time I saw her bathing in the river Tiber; and I gave her my hand, and led her out of the river. So, seeing her beauty, I reasoned in my heart, saying, "Happy were I, if I had such a one to wife both in beauty and in character." I merely reflected on this and nothing more. After a certain time, as I was journeying to Cumae, and glorifying God's creatures for their greatness and splendor and power, as I walked I fell asleep. And a Spirit took me, and bore me away through a pathless tract, through which no man could pass: for the place was precipitous, and broken into clefts by reason of the waters. When then I had crossed the river, I came into the level country, and knelt down, and began to pray to the Lord and to confess my sins. Now, while I prayed, the heaven was opened, and I see the lady, whom I had desired, greeting me from heaven, saying, "Good morrow, Hermas." And, looking at her, I said to her, "Lady, what doest thou here?" Then she answered me, "I was taken up, that I might convict thee of thy sins before the Lord.[30]""

While this is just a sample passage, it is symptomatic of the entire book which contains apocalyptic visions but little or no reference to historic people or events. By comparison, even the apocalyptic book of Revelation couches the visions in historical context and contains direct messages to the churches at that time in history.

Non-Biblical Historic text

It is worthwhile, then, to make the comparison between the Biblical passages cited above and a passage from the first century Jewish historian, Flavius Josephus:

"Now Cumanus, and the principal of the Samaritans, who were sent to Rome, had a day appointed them by the emperor whereon they were to have pleaded their cause about the quarrels they had one with another. But now Caesar's freed-men and his friends were very zealous on the behalf of Cumanus and the Samaritans; and they had prevailed over the Jews, unless Agrippa, junior, who was then at Rome, had seen the principal of the Jews hard set, and had earnestly entreated Agrippina, the emperor's wife, to persuade her husband to hear the cause, so as was agreeable to his justice, and to condemn those to be punished who were really the authors of this revolt from the Roman government: - whereupon Claudius was so well disposed beforehand, that when he had heard the cause, and found that the Samaritans had been the ringleaders in those mischievous doings, he gave order that those who came up to him should be slain, and that Cureanus should be banished.[31]"

When placed side-by-side, the New Testament documents read much more like history than they do religious fantasy.

New Testament claims to be eyewitness testimony

It is necessary to note that the authors of the New Testament documents claim to be writing real history. In the Gospel of Luke, for instance, the author writes:

"Inasmuch as many have undertaken to compile a narrative of the things that have been accomplished among us, just as those who from the beginning were eyewitnesses and ministers of the word have delivered them to us," (Luke 1:1-2 ESV)

In the first epistle of John, the author says:

"That which was from the beginning, which we have heard, which we have seen with our eyes, which we have looked upon, and our hands have handled, concerning the Word of life—the life was manifested, and we have seen, and bear witness, and declare to you that eternal life which was with the Father and was manifest to us—that which we have seen and heard we declare to you, that you also may have fellowship with us. ..." (1 John 1:1-2 ESV)

In his second epistle, Apostle Peter writes:

"For we did not follow cleverly devised myths when we made known to you the power and coming of our Lord Jesus Christ, but we were eyewitnesses of his majesty." (2 Peter 1:16 ESV)

And in his letter to the Corinthians, Paul delivers the message of salvation in distinctly historical terms:

"For I delivered to you as of first importance what I also received: that Christ died for our sins in accordance with the Scriptures, 4 that he was buried, that he was raised on the third day in accordance with the Scriptures, 5 and that he appeared to Cephas, then to the twelve. 6 Then he appeared to more than five hundred brothers at one time, most of whom are still alive, though some have fallen asleep. [7] Then he appeared to James, then to all the apostles. [8] Last of all, as to one untimely born, he appeared also to me." (1 Corinthians 15:3-8 ESV)

Taken on its own terms, the New Testament claims to be a historical account. To eliminate it from the historical milieu based on the fact that it falls under the category of "religious" or because it contains accounts of the miraculous is to neatly dodge the consequence of seriously considering the evidence it presents. That consequence being: it just might be true.

Historic accuracy of Luke

The Gospel of Luke has undergone a great deal of attack over the years, mainly because it includes so many specific historical details. Critics have picked at these details from every angle possible in an attempt to discredit the book. For years, especially in the nineteenth century, *Luke* was considered to be a cesspool of historical errors.

However, as archeology in the Middle East has advanced, the historical accuracies of *Luke* and *Acts* have been repeatedly confirmed.

Renowned archeologist Sir William Ramsey (1852-1916), a vehement critic of the authenticity of the Bible, spent a good portion of his career attempting to discredit the writings of Luke. After fifteen years, he was forced to admit, "Luke is a historian of the first rank.... This author should be placed along with the very greatest of historians.[32]"

Scholar Stephen Neil makes this observation concerning Luke's writings:

"The writer of Acts knew the correct titles and used them with varying precision. In the words of Ramsey: 'The officials with whom Paul and his companions were brought into contact are those who would be there. Every person is found just where he ought to be; proconsuls in senatorial provinces, asiarchs in Ephesus, strategoi in Philippi, politarchs in Thessalonica, magicians and soothsayers everywhere.' The Most remarkable of these titles is Politarch the ruler of the city used in Acts 17:6 ... previously this word had been completely unknown except for this passage in Acts. It has now been found in 19 inscriptions dating from the second century...[33]"

In fact, the word "politarch" was only ever used to refer to local officials in Thessalonica during a certain period in history, making the word choice extremely precise.

This is why *Luke* is also a very important book. For every detail of the book that can be confirmed, the overall accuracy of his message becomes more and more apparent.

Who wrote *Luke* and *Acts*?

Determining the author of *Luke* is not as important as the other three gospels, because the author is clearly not an eyewitness. The author is a biographer and historian, so the question is not who wrote it, but rather is the author accurate in his facts?

The authorship of the Gospel of Luke is inferred from the fact that *Luke* and *Acts* clearly had the same author based on the preface and writing styles of the two books, and based on the fact that one picks up where the other left off.

Since the book of *Acts* continually slips into the first person plural for stories in which Luke is included, and because Luke was a companion of Paul and Paul quotes from Luke's gospel twice in his epistles, scholars infer that Luke was most likely the author of the Gospel.

What makes *Luke* different from the other gospels?

Luke makes it clear from the outset that his intention is to write an orderly and accurate account of the life of Christ. Mark's account is a very broken and disordered account. Matthew's account orders events in a thematic fashion, arranging all of Jesus' parables and sermons in subsections. Luke's attention to detail and the preface to his book indicate that he felt the need to order the events of Jesus' life chronologically. Luke never makes claims to be an eyewitness, and appears to use *Matthew* and *Mark* as references for his gospel; it can be assumed that the author is *not* an eyewitness. However, Luke claims to have access to eyewitnesses:

Luke 1:2
English Standard Version (ESV)

Just as those who from the beginning were eyewitnesses and ministers of the word have delivered them to us

For the purposes of this section, the primary point that we will address is that Luke had access to accurate reports that reveal what the eyewitnesses would have seen. In the process, we will look at some of the criticisms Luke has faced, and the answers to these criticisms. If *Luke* can be shown to be accurate in its historical details, it is more likely that the unusual information that it relates—miracles and Jesus' resurrection—are also accurate.

Note that the following arguments are not offered to categorically defeat the criticisms leveled against *Luke*, but rather to provide reasonable responses that uphold the overall accuracy of *Luke*. Every criticism has a reasonable response, whether or not the critics accept them.

The Census

There are five verses in Luke that are more disputed than practically any other passage in his writings. Luke 2:1-5 reads like this:

> "In those days a decree went out from Caesar Augustus that all the world should be registered. [2] This was the first registration when Quirinius was governor of Syria. [3] And all went to be registered, each to his own town. [4] And Joseph also went up from Galilee, from the town of Nazareth, to Judea, to the city of David, which is called Bethlehem, because he was of the house and lineage of David, [5] to be registered with Mary, his betrothed, who was with child."

This passage lays out some fairly specific historical details, which is why it is so heavily attacked. Skeptics will argue that Luke got practically every detail wrong. On the one hand, Caesar Augustus never issued a decree to take a census of the Roman Empire; on the other hand, he would not have ordered such a census in just Herod's domain, as that would be Herod's job.

Even if Caesar *had* commanded such a census, it would make no sense for a Roman to command Jews to register at their ancestral home, there would be no way to enforce or even know if they had actually registered at the correct location, and such a mass migration of people to different towns would have been untenable, chaotic, and economically disastrous.

Additionally, Luke seems to be playing fast and loose with chronological events. Quirinius wasn't elected governor of Syria until six years after Herod the Great was dead, but according to the book of Matthew, Herod the Great was a major player in the events surrounding Jesus' birth. Jesus was supposedly born sometime around 7-5 BCE, but Quirinius was elected around CE 12[34].

A decree went out from Caesar Augustus that all the world should be registered ...

A good deal of the objections related to the census have to do with a biased reading of the text that ignores certain historical facts. In the last years of his reign, Herod the Great fell into disfavor with Rome. Jewish historian Josephus records that Augustus sent a letter to Herod:

> *Cæsar [Augustus] ... grew very angry, and wrote to Herod sharply. The sum of his epistle was this, that whereas of old he used him as a friend, he should now use him as his subject."* *(Josephus, Antiquities 16.9.3 (#290)).*

Herod was demoted from *rex socius* to *rex amicus*. Not only would this have given Caesar the direct authority to tax Judea, but in order to regain favor with Augustus, Herod's entire empire was required to swear allegiance to Rome, which may well explain the registration[34]. As Josephus tells it:

> *Accordingly, when all the people of the Jews gave assurance of their goodwill to Cæsar [Augustus], and to the king's [Herod's] government, these very men [the Pharisees] did not swear, being above six thousand. (Josephus, "Ant.", XVII, ii, 4)*

More than this, however, it is historically verifiable that Rome did, in fact, have an ongoing census that occurred throughout the Roman Empire. In his book *Archeology of the New Testament*, historian R.K. Harrison writes,

> *Sir William Ramsay showed that, based upon the word used in Luke, Cesar Augustus laid down the requirements for an ongoing census not one massive poll taking. That the machinery for such an undertaking was in operation at the time is found in the Works of Clement of Alexandria (155-202) who recorded that it commenced with the census that was in progress at the time when Christ was born. Documentary evidence from Egypt*

consisting of actual census reports for enrolments in AD 90, 104, 118, 132, and succeeding years is now at hand, and it is an accredited fact that in the latter empire there was a 14-year interval between enrolments. [Harrison, p.22, 23]

This evidence lays the foundation for the case that the census to which Luke refers was simply the latest in the ongoing census Rome kept of the empire. Taking both of these historic facts into consideration makes Luke's account seem historically sound.

But what of the apparent requirement for the Jews to return to their ancestral home?

The Mosaic book of *Numbers* records the very first census of the Jewish people:

Numbers 1:1-4
English Standard Version (ESV)

1 The LORD spoke to Moses in the wilderness of Sinai, in the tent of meeting, on the first day of the second month, in the second year after they had come out of the land of Egypt, saying, ² "Take a census of all the congregation of the people of Israel, by clans, by fathers' houses, according to the number of names, every male, head by head. ³ From twenty years old and upward, all in Israel who are able to go to war, you and Aaron shall list them, company by company. ⁴ And there shall be with you a man from each tribe, each man being the head of the house of his fathers.

This account seems to set the standard for a Jewish census. Notice that both Matthew and Luke go to great lengths to trace Jesus' genealogy not through Mary, who was his biological parent, but through Joseph, who was the head of the household. The Jewish people were very concerned with lineage and genealogy throughout their history. While one might not be able to force citizens to register at their ancestral home, Jews would most likely consider it a matter of pride and honor to register where their ancestors were prominent. We know from Matthew's account that Joseph was an honorable man and a devout Jew (Matthew 1:19). He most likely would have made the journey even if not compelled to do so, but as a matter of familial pride.

Moreover, it is not as untenable as it may seem to have the Jews return to their ancestral home. Massive migrations and pilgrimages were a common thing throughout Israel's history. Every year, thousands of faithful Jews made the journey to Jerusalem to make sacrifices and worship at the temple, and to celebrate high holy days such as Passover and Pentecost. In fact, this kind of travel appears to have been beneficial to the economy of Judea, as the travelers would have to pay for lodging and supplies.

Archeology provides further proof for this method of census. A manuscript from Egypt dated to CE 104 reads:

C. Vibius Maximus, Prefect of Egypt, gives notice:

The enrollment by household being at hand, it is necessary to notify all who for any cause whatsoever are outside their nomes (administrative divisions of Egypt) *to return to their domestic hearths, that they may also accomplish the customary dispensation of enrollment and continue steadfastly in the husbandry that belongs to them*[35].

As shown by this document, the Roman census appears to have required people to return to their place of origin in order to register.

But why should Rome institute a census according to Jewish methods?

In the Roman census papers that archeologists uncovered from Egypt, it appears that the Romans polled each household by the name and age of the (male) head of the household, who would list the name and age of his wife, children, servants, and any additions to the household since the last census. The Jewish census as described in *Numbers* was concerned only with the male heads of household, and organized them by tribe, clan, and family.

The region of Judea was an especially unstable one, and the Romans went to great pains to allow the Jewish people the autonomy to practice their traditions as freely as was possible while still paying tribute to Rome.

It is not unusual, then, that Rome would have deferred to the Jewish method of census. It gave them the information they required for taxation purposes, and allowed the Jews to track tribe and lineage, which was specifically a Jewish concern. In fact, this may have been used as a motivation to encourage Jews to comply, as it seems unlikely that they would enthusiastically swear allegiance to Rome or give Rome information to help in taxing them.

This was the first registration when Quirinius was governor of Syria ...

Luke states that "This was the first registration when Quirinius was governor of Syria." This seems to run counter to the known historic facts of the time. According to other sources, Quirinius was not elected governor of Syria until CE 6, ten years after Herod the Great had died. After Quirinius became governor, he issued a taxation of the region that is well documented. This has led skeptics to the conclusion that Luke is citing the well-known taxation Quirinius levied in CE 6, getting his facts wrong by an embarrassing ten years[34].

It is worth noting that Luke knew about the taxation of CE 6 as he references it in passing in the book of Acts (5:37). Luke also shows awareness that Jesus was born during the reign of Herod the Great, as he cites Herod's reign in the first chapter of Luke (vs. 5). This makes Luke's account consistent with Matthews.

So if Luke is aware that the taxation under Quirinius took place in CE 6, and that Jesus was born around 6BCE under the reign of Herod the Great, and if Luke is such a careful historian, why the historical blunder?

In his lecture series, "Reliability of the Gospels[34]," Dr. Tim McGrew makes it clear that the Greek reading of the passage does not clearly state that the taxation Luke is referring to is the one that takes place in CE 6. Instead, the Greek appears to say that the people were required to *register*, whereas what occurred in CE 6 was an actual taxation.

If Quirinius used the information gained in the registration of 6BCE in order to carry out his taxation in CE 6, this may very well explain why Luke references him. Luke is essentially saying that the data from the *registration* of 6BCE led to the *taxation* of Quirinus' reign in CE 6. In fact, the Greek construction of the sentence is a bit awkward, and could easily be rendered, "This is the first registration *before* Quirinius was governor of Syria.[34]" Translated this way, it removes any objection.

There is, however, another potential solution. Scholars have suggested that Quirinius may have served two separate terms as governor of Syria under extraordinary circumstances[34]. Such unusual arrangements were not uncommon at the time. For instance, Josephus mentions a cogovernor of Syria in one of his writings[34]. There is also some archeological support for this idea. An inscription discovered at Tivoli reads, "being a legate of Augustus for the second time received Syria and Phoenecia.[34]"

The name is missing from the inscription, but if this is referring to Quirinius, it may be the explanation for Luke's citation.

Another piece of archeological evidence for the possible dual reign of Quirinius is a coin discovered by archeologist Jerry Vardaman that has Quirinius's name engraved on it. Vardaman says that the coin would place him as a proconsul of Syria and Cilicia from 11BCE until the death of Herod[36].

Jesus' childhood

Luke's narrative starts earlier than the other Gospels, with the story surrounding the conception of John the Baptist and of Jesus. Since many of the stories unique to Luke's Gospel appear to be told from Mary's perspective, many speculate that Luke had access to Mary as a source[37]. Not only this, but Luke's narrative focuses on the female followers of Jesus more than any of the other gospels. As an example:

- Luke uses words such as "women" and "womb" more times than the other Gospels
- Only Luke is interested in Mary's inner life (2:18, 34, 51)
- Luke writes the famous lines rejoicing in pregnancy (1:42-46)
- Luke is the only author to mention fetal quickening and mentions it as a symptom of the Holy Spirit coming into the womb (1:42)
- Luke implies that Jesus' female companions outnumbered his male companions (8:2)
- Luke tells of the women being first at the tomb
- Luke tells in *Acts* that the first European Christian was a woman

Given these facts, it is not outside the realm of possibility that Luke did extensive interviews with Jesus' female followers for many of his facts.

It is also possible that his source for Jesus' birth and childhood stories were James or Jude, half-brothers of Jesus who were influential in the early church and most likely heard these accounts from their mother. Since Joseph disappears from the Gospel narratives fairly early, and since Jesus hands responsibility for Mary's care over to John at the cross (John 19:25-27), it is likely that Joseph died early, which makes it all the more likely that the brothers of Jesus would have heard the stories from their mother's perspective rather than their father's.

Here is a list of stories found only in *Luke* that appear to be from Mary's point of view. Notice the large number of details from Jesus' childhood, especially those that would have had an impact on a young mother:

- The prophecy and conception of John the Baptist. Mary knew Elizabeth and visited her shortly after she knew she was pregnant, so Mary would have heard the story of John's conception
- The visitation of Gabriel to Mary. Matthew contains the birth narrative from Joseph's perspective. Luke gives us Mary's perspective.
- Mary's visit to Elizabeth and her *Magnificat* (prophetic song of praise)
- The birth of John the Baptist
- The prophecy of Zechariah (John's father)
- Summary of John's childhood
- The census and trip from Nazareth to Bethlehem
- The very intimate details of Jesus' birth, including the location of the birth (a stable) and his swaddling and bedding
- The visit of the shepherd and Mary's personal reaction to the visit: *"But Mary treasured up all these things and pondered them in her heart"* (Luke 2:19)
- Jesus' circumcision
- Jesus' dedication at the temple, the prophecy of Simeon, and Joseph and Mary's reaction to the prophecy *"And his father and his mother marveled at what was said about him"* (Luke 2:33). This section also includes a personal conversation between Simeon and Mary that, among other things, foretells Jesus' crucifixion and it's emotional impact on Mary specifically: *"And Simeon*

blessed them and said to Mary his mother, 'Behold, this child is appointed for the fall and rising of many in Israel, and for a sign that is opposed (and a sword will pierce through your own soul also), so that thoughts from many hearts may be revealed.'" (Luke 2:34-35)

- The prophecy of Anna in the temple
- Jesus as a boy teaching in the temple "And he went down with them and came to Nazareth and was submissive to them. *And his mother treasured up all these things in her heart"* (Luke 2:51). Once again, notice the emphasis on Mary's reaction
- Summary of Jesus' growth to adulthood

All of the events summarized here are consistent with what a mother would have focused on when recounting the story of her child's birth and childhood. Luke writes a very compelling account of what a mother might say about her exceptional child.

The Rise of John the Baptist

After Luke's summary of Jesus' childhood, he transitions into the rise of John the Baptist. In a manner typical of Luke, he starts by framing John's ministry in historic context:

Luke 3:1-3
English Standard Version (ESV)

John the Baptist Prepares the Way

3 In the fifteenth year of the reign of Tiberius Caesar, Pontius Pilate being governor of Judea, and Herod being tetrarch of Galilee, and his brother Philip tetrarch of the region of Ituraea and Trachonitis, and Lysanias tetrarch of Abilene, [2] during the high priesthood of Annas and Caiaphas, the word of God came to John the son of Zechariah in the wilderness.[3] And he went into all the region around the Jordan, proclaiming a baptism of repentance for the forgiveness of sins.

Keeping in mind that at the time Luke was writing there was no standard system of dating, it is likely that Luke references the various rulers in order to give the reader a precise idea of when these events took place. But here, once again, critics will attack what Luke has said.

"Governor" Pontius Pilate

Firstly, the word Luke uses to refer to Pontius Pilate is "governor" (ἡγεμών). In fact, Pilate was in a station a little more elevated than governor. He was technically a "prefect" (νομάρχης). Was this another historic blunder on Luke's part?

Actually, this is just what it is described to be: a technicality. Even though Pilate was a prefect, it was not uncommon to refer to him as a governor, nor is Luke the only writer to do so. Both Josephus, the Jewish historian, and Tacitus, the Roman historian, use the same term when referring to Pilate[34].

Lysanias, tetrarch of Abilene ...

Perhaps a more powerful objection to this passage is Luke's reference to Lysanias, tetrarch of Abilene. According to Josephus, Lysanias was tetrarch from 40 to 36 BCE. This would make Luke's dating off by an embarrassing 60 years[34].

Here, once again, archeology comes to the rescue. A temple inscription from the time of Tiberius reads:

> *For the salvation of the August lords and of all their household, Nymphaeus, freedman of Eagle Lysanias tetrarch, established this street and other things. –[Corpus Inscriptionum Graecarum 4521*

"August Lords" is a title that was only ever used to refer to Tiberius and Livia who was the widow of Tiberius' predecessor and retained her title from when her husband was alive. Since Livia's husband died in CE 14 and Livia herself died in CE 29, this inscription has to date somewhere in this time. The inscription names Lysanias as tetrarch, just as Luke does. The Lysanias mentioned by Josephus is clearly a different individual from the one that Luke and the inscription indicate[34].

During the high priesthood of Annas and Caiaphas

In verse 2, both Annas and Caiaphas are listed as the High Priest. Only one person could hold the office of High Priest at a time, and it was a lifelong post. Some will criticize *Luke's* accuracy or knowledge of Jewish customs because he references two High Priests when there could only be one.

This is explained easily enough. Annas was elected High Priest in CE 6 by Quirinius. He was subsequently disposed from his position in CE 15 by the Roman procurator, Gratus, who accused him of "imposing and executing capital sentences which had been forbidden by the imperial government.[38]"

After CE 15, several High Priests were elected and disposed and finally Caiaphas was elected in 18CE. So far as the Romans were concerned, Caiaphas was the High Priest. However, since Annas had not yet died, Jewish tradition still held him as High Priest. By citing both of them, Luke is accurately pinpointing the time period by both Roman and Jewish estimation [34].

The synagogue at Capernaum ...

A demonstration of the bias of those who examine the gospels is that, rather than taking into account the many historic and archeological proofs of the accuracy of Luke as evidence that other material in the book must also be accurate, they begin with the assumption that the material is inaccurate and that anything in which the book matches historic fact is an anomaly. As a result, they jump on anything the book says that runs counter to what they currently know of history. Unfortunately for them, in almost every instance, archeological discoveries confirm Luke's account.

An example of this would be an account from Luke 7:1-5, which reads:

Luke 7:1-5
English Standard Version (ESV)

Jesus Heals a Centurion's Servant

7 After he had finished all his sayings in the hearing of the people, he entered Capernaum. ² Now a centurion had a servant who was sick and at the point of death, who was highly valued by him. ³ When the centurion heard about Jesus, he sent to him elders of the Jews, asking him to come and heal his servant. ⁴ And when they came to Jesus, they pleaded with him earnestly, saying, "He is worthy to have you do this for him, ⁵ for he loves our nation, and he is the one who built us our synagogue."

In this passage, the Jews mentioned that the centurion had built them a synagogue. However, critics say that while these Jews were in Capernaum, there were no synagogues in the Galilean region until the pharisaic sects were forced to flee there after CE 70 when the Romans raided Jerusalem. This was another instance in which the critics said that Luke got his facts wrong and displayed his historic ignorance. Says critic Robert M. Price:

A major collision between the gospel tradition and archaeology concerns the existence of synagogues and Pharisees in pre-70 C.E. Galilee. Historical logic implies that there would not have been any, since Pharisees fled to Galilee only after the fall of Jerusalem.[39]

In the 1980s, however, archeologists uncovered the foundation of a synagogue from the first century that had quite clearly been an impressive structure. The building had over 450 square feet of interior space and had walls over 3 feet thick. An archeology journal dated from 1983 stated:

> The first-century Capernaum synagogue in which Jesus preached has probably been found. Because more than one synagogue may have existed in Capernaum at this time, we cannot be sure that this new find was Jesus' synagogue. But this recently discovered first-century building is certainly a likely candidate.... The conclusion that this was a first-century A.D. synagogue seems inescapable.[40]

Once again, archeology appears to agree with Luke.

Jesus' journey to Jerusalem

One final criticism of the book of Luke we will examine concerns Jesus' journey to Jerusalem as recorded in Luke 17:11:

Luke 17:11
English Standard Version (ESV)

[11] On the way to Jerusalem he was passing along between Samaria and Galilee.

Critics rarely acknowledge the accurate geography within the gospels and Acts, but when something appears to be off, as it does here, they are quick to leap at the fact.

In this instance, if Jesus was headed to Jerusalem, he was taking an extremely inconvenient route to do so. Since Samaria lies *between* Galilee and Judea, why would Jesus skirt the border rather than take the straight route through Samaria?

In point of fact, there is a fairly obvious explanation for this: at this point in history, the region of Samaria was unstable and hostile. Earlier in the book of Luke, Samaritans had outright refused to welcome Jesus because they find out he is traveling to Jerusalem:

> **Luke 9:51-56**
> English Standard Version (ESV)
>
> **A Samaritan Village Rejects Jesus**
>
> [51] When the days drew near for him to be taken up, he set his face to go to Jerusalem. [52] And he sent messengers ahead of him, who went and entered a village of the Samaritans, to make preparations for him. [53] But the people did not receive him, because his face was set toward Jerusalem. [54] And when his disciples James and John saw it, they said, "Lord, do you want us to tell fire to come down from heaven and consume them?" [55] But he turned and rebuked them. [56] And they went on to another village.

This rejection from Samaritans may have been influential in Jesus' decision not to travel through that region.

In CE 52, about two decades after Christ died, Samaritans killed a number of Jewish pilgrims from Galilee who were foolish enough to take the direct route to Jerusalem.[34] This action simply reinforces the danger of Jewish pilgrims traveling to Jerusalem through the Samaritan region.

The route that Jesus and his disciples chose would also have kept them close to freshwater for the duration of the journey.

Summary

Throughout this section, we have looked at the critical objections to the Gospel of Luke, and how a close examination of these objections actually confirms the historicity of Luke's Gospel.

Luke appears not just to be a person writing in the same time period that his story takes place, but a very informed person at that.

One could still argue that he used his knowledge of the era and area in which he lived to write an imaginative fiction. But in order to make this claim, the critic is forced to cast off the notion that the stories of Jesus' resurrection and miraculous nature was a late invention that gradually got exaggerated over several centuries. Either Luke was extremely well-informed about an era in the past that he did not actually live through, but was simultaneously fooled into believing a mythical character from that same time period, or he was a man who lived in the same period of history about which he was writing and used his well-informed mind to craft a clever lie. The former seems ridiculous since such a well-informed and meticulous man should probably have seen through mythology to the truth, to say nothing of the fact that the story does not read like mythology. If the latter was the case, many people from the same time period should have seen through his lie by falsifying contemporary events he cites.

Chapter 10
EVIDENCE FOR THE BOOK OF *JOHN*

The Gospel of John, as mentioned previously, is largely considered to be a late addition to the New Testament. Critics will place it as much as several centuries after the events it claims to relate[41]. There are several reasons for this.

The book of John appears to have "High Christology"—that is, it portrays Christ as being equal to God, and clearly relates a message of salvation from sins through faith. Critics will make the claim that the other gospels reflect a "Low Christology"—that is, they portray Christ as a social reformer whose primary teaching has to do with care for the needy and love of one's neighbor, and equality among individuals. These critics tend to say that this reflects a more accurate concept of who the historical Jesus was and what he said, and that the concept of Jesus-as-God and salvation from sins through faith was a later invention of Apostle Paul. Since the message of John's Gospel seems to correlate with the teaching of salvation by Paul, critics will say that it must have been written by later Christians who were already sold on this distinctly Christian idea[17].

Another thing that separates John's Gospel from the others is the fact that it contains a number of stories that are unique to that gospel. Whereas Matthew, Mark, and Luke tend to repeat most of the same information, John's gospel tells new stories about Jesus not seen in the others. Whereas critics will claim that the other gospels are probably all drawing from the same primitive traditions, explaining their similarities, they will tend to say that *John* is making up new stories about Jesus that are more in line with what the later church taught.

A third point critics will bring against the book of John is the *person* of John. *John* is the only gospel that contains a "signature." Throughout the book, John refers to himself as "the disciple that Jesus loved," and at the end of the book, he essentially tells the reader that he, John, is the author of the book:

John 21:20-24
English Standard Version (ESV)

Jesus and the Beloved Apostle

[20] Peter turned and saw the disciple whom Jesus loved following them, the one who also had leaned back against him during the supper and had said, "Lord, who is it that is going to betray you?" [21] When Peter saw him, he said to Jesus, "Lord, what about this man?" [22] Jesus said to him, "If it is my will that he remain until I come, what is that to you? You follow me!" [23] So the saying spread abroad among the brothers that this disciple was not to die; yet Jesus did not say to him that he was not to die, but, "If it is my will that he remain until I come, what is that to you?"

[24] This is the disciple who is bearing witness about these things, and who has written these things, and we know that his testimony is true.

Since John was one of the most prominent disciples and leaders of the early church, he would be a natural choice (critics claim) to whom one might credit a forged gospel.

Taken together, the argument is that someone in the later Christian Church forged a gospel that more clearly reflected the High Christology that had developed over several centuries and then very clearly credited the gospel to a prominent disciple and church leader.

Here we will examine the evidence that John's Gospel is based on eyewitness accounts.

External Evidence

Early references to *John*

The Gospel of John was quoted from or alluded to in church writings very early on. The following is a list of early writers who reference *John* in their documents[42]:

- Ignatius (c. 70CE)
- Justin Martyr (probably) (c. 130CE)
- Tatian (c. 150CE)
- Basilides (c.120CE)
- Valentinus (c. 130CE)

Irenaeus - c. 130-210CE

In the late second century, a bishop named Irenaeus from Asia Minor wrote a five-volume work refuting the heresy of Gnosticism. In this book, Irenaeus shares that he grew up under the tutelage of a man named Polycarp. Polycarp was, in turn, a disciple of Apostle John. Both Apostle John and his disciple Polycarp lived to be very old, so there is no reason to doubt Irenaeus's claim. In his works, Irenaeus states that John wrote the Gospel during his residence at Ephesus in Asia Minor when he was advanced in age (*Against Heresies* 2.22.5; 3.1.1). Since Irenaeus had a secondhand account of John's teaching, this seems like strong evidence not only that John's Gospel is not a late mythology, but that it was actually written by John himself.

Clement of Alexandria- c. 150-215CE

Clement wrote that John, aware of the facts set forth in the other Gospels and being moved by the Holy Spirit, composed a "Spiritual Gospel" (see Eusebius's *Ecclesiastical History* 6.14.7)

Other writers:

Authorship of the gospel was directly attributed to John by[42]:

- Theophilus, Bishop of Antioch - 180CE
- Tertullian (c.200CE)
- The Muratoriun fragment (probably around 170CE)

Archeology

The Bethesda Pool

The Gospel of John contains the only account we have of the pool at Bethesda, described this way:

John 5:2
English Standard Version (ESV)

"Now there is in Jerusalem by the Sheep Gate a pool, in Aramaic called Bethesda, which has five roofed colonnades."

For years, this account was criticized as fanciful fiction as scholars said that no such structure ever existed. In the nineteenth century, however, this exact structure, just as John described it, was unearthed exactly where John described it would be. The discovery of this pool destroyed one of the classic arguments skeptics used to support the idea that John was a late mythology.

Egyptian Fragment

P52. By Raxom (Own work) [CC-BY-SA-3.0 or GFDL], via Wikimedia Commons

In 1920, a fragment of John 18:31-33 and John 18:37-38 was discovered in Egypt. Labeled P52, objective dating methods place this fragment between 90 to 150CE. This is the earliest discovered fragmentary manuscript of the New Testament, predating the earliest known copies of the other three gospels and all of the epistles. Considering that it would take a significant amount of time for copies of John's gospel to circulate from its point of origin

(Ephesus) to southern Egypt, this places the original writing of John at least decades earlier than this.

Testament of Critics

In his lecture series *The Quest: The Historian's Search for Jesus and Muhammad*, scholar F. E. Peters, who is no conservative, points out that despite critics' attack on the Gospel of John for high Christology, those same critics will generally agree that Paul's epistles were written *before* the gospels. It is difficult to support the claim that because of its high Christology, John must be a late addition when the earliest Christian writings *already display* a high Christology. The concept of Jesus as Savior manifests itself in writing within thirty years of Jesus' death!

Internal Evidence

John is a *very* evidential book. Whereas Matthew and Mark focus on Jesus' miracles, and Luke focuses on his teaching, John structures his book so that the miracles *support* the teaching. This follows the biblical formula that direct messages from God are always accompanied by miracles in order to prove their legitimacy.

John is also the only book that records the "doubting Thomas" episode (20:24-29), where one of the disciples requires direct physical evidence as support to Jesus' resurrection rather than just accepting the overwhelming eyewitness testimony. John undoubtedly had the Thomas story in mind when he said, in 1 John, "That which was from the beginning, which we have heard, which we have seen with our eyes, which we have looked upon, and our hands have handled, concerning the Word of life—the life was manifested, and we have seen, and bear witness, and declare to you that eternal life which was with the Father and was manifest to us—that which we have seen and heard we declare to you, that you also may have fellowship with us...." (1 John 1:1-2)

The fact that John's book is intended as evidence to the legitimacy of Christ is reaffirmed both by several verses within the book (20:31; 21:24; 2:22), and by John's statement in his first epistle (1:1-3).

The fact that the Gospel of John differs so greatly from the other Gospels, yet was accepted unanimously by the early church fathers, reinforces the idea that they knew Apostle John was the author. By contrast, false gospels sprang up all over during the first centuries and were unanimously rejected by the early Church fathers.

One can trace the history of early church thought and evangelism through the focus of each gospel. Mark's gospel was thrown together relatively quickly to get the essential details of Jesus's life and ministry out to the growing number of early churches. Matthew's gospel was written as an apologetic to the Jewish people to persuade them that Jesus was, in fact, their Messiah. Luke, written later, is an attempt to create an orderly, historical account of Jesus's life.

As the decades passed, the church began to realize that Christ may not be returning as soon as they originally thought. The eyewitnesses to Jesus's life and ministry were all dying off, and the church was passing into the hands of a new generation. The early seeds of heresy were beginning to spring up, and John, no doubt, saw the urgent need to reinforce the concrete, evidential nature of Jesus before he died. The book of John strains to tell its readers that this is the truth and the truth was witnessed in a real way.

Within the book of John, it is fairly apparent that the disciple John was the author, using this chain of evidence[43]:

1.) The author was probably a Jew as the style of writing, the vocabulary, the familiarity with Jewish customs and characteristics, and the background of the Old Testament suggest.

111

2.) He was a Jew who lived in Palestine (1:28; 2:1, 11; 4:46; 11:18, 54; 21:1, 2). He knew both Jerusalem and the temple intimately (5:2; 9:7; 18:1; 19:13, 17, 20, 41; also see 2:14-16; 8:20; 10:22)

3.) He was an eyewitness of the events he is narrating, as seen by the specific details concerning people, places, and historical details (4:46; 5:14; 6:59; 12:21; 13:1; 14:5, 8; 18:6; 19:31).

4.) He was an apostle as shown by his intimate knowledge of the inner circle and of Jesus (6:19, 60, 61; 12:16; 13:22, 28; 16:19)

5.) Whereas Matthew, Mark, and Luke identify the disciple John by name approximately twenty times, the author of *John* does not, instead calling him "the disciple that Jesus loved" (13:23; 19:26; 21:7, 20). By process of elimination, then, the author *must have been* John.

The fact that John calls himself "the disciple that Jesus loved" rather than by his actual name is significant because it reflects his humility and direct relationship with Christ.

The book makes several claims that the author is, in fact, an eyewitness:

John 1:14
English Standard Version (ESV)

¹⁴ And the Word became flesh and dwelt among us, and *we have seen his glory*, glory as of the only Son from the Father, full of grace and truth.

John 19:35
English Standard Version (ESV)

[35] He who saw it has borne witness—his testimony is true, and he knows that he is telling the truth—that you also may believe.

John 21:24
English Standard Version (ESV)

[24] This is the disciple who is bearing witness about these things, and who has written these things, and we know that his testimony is true.

Summary

The evidence suggests that John was written later than the other Gospels, by John to a church that was about half a century old. That John knew about the other Gospels, and wrote his not to echo the information already provided by the other three Gospels. John's gospel was written by an elderly man to a generation that no longer had access to the direct eyewitnesses of Christ. He is urging this generation to faithfulness to the message by stressing that the eyewitness testimony was true and that Christ preached repentance from sin and salvation through faith, consistent with the message of the apostles. His Gospel refines and clarifies some of the content found in the other books.

Chapter 11
INTERTESTIMONIAL SUPPORT

I n his book, *Cold Case Christianity*, Homicide Detective J. Warner Wallace tells of a time when he arrived at a crime scene after the regular police had already responded. It was raining hard, and the police officer who was first on the scene had rounded up the witnesses and put them in the back of the police car to keep them out of the rain. In so-doing, the officer had unwittingly damaged the eyewitness testimony. When Wallace interviewed the witnesses, all of their stories sounded the same. Why? Because when they were together in the car, they had talked to one another and their stories synced up.

In order to investigate the crime, Wallace was counting on each eyewitness telling the story from their point of view. By looking at the *differences* in the stories, Wallace would have been able to gain a better idea of what had actually happened. When the stories synced, they had lost their nuance and damaged the case[44].

If the Gospels are eyewitness testimonies, one would expect the same kinds of nuance that is true of other kinds of eyewitness testimony. And in fact, this is exactly what we find.

In his book, *Undesigned Scriptural Coincidences*, scholar J.J. Blunt (2005) lists an enormous number of events recorded in scripture that unintentionally support one another, just as one would expect from several eyewitnesses reporting the same event. Here are a few examples:

The Calling of the first disciples:

Matthew 4:18-22
English Standard Version (ESV)

Jesus Calls the First Disciples

[18] While walking by the Sea of Galilee, he saw two brothers, Simon (who is called Peter) and Andrew his brother, casting a net into the sea, for they were fishermen. [19] And he said to them, "Follow me, and I will make you fishers of men." [20] Immediately they left their nets and followed him. [21] And going on from there he saw two other brothers, James the son of Zebedee and John his brother, in the boat with Zebedee their father, *mending their nets*, and he called them. [22] Immediately they left the boat and their father and followed him.

Luke 5:1-10
English Standard Version (ESV)

Jesus Calls the First Disciples

5 On one occasion, while the crowd was pressing in on him to hear the word of God, he was standing by the lake of Gennesaret, [2] and he saw two boats by the lake, but the fishermen had gone out of them and were washing their nets. [3] Getting into one of the boats, which was Simon's, he asked him to put out a little from the land. And he sat down and taught the people from the boat. [4] And when he had finished speaking, he said to Simon, "Put out into the deep and let down your nets for a catch." [5] And Simon answered, "Master, we toiled all night and took nothing! But at your word I will let down the nets." [6] And when they had done this, they enclosed a large number of fish, *and their nets were breaking.* [7] They signaled to their partners in the other boat to come and help them. And they came and filled both the boats, so that they began to sink. [8] But when Simon Peter saw it, he fell down at Jesus' knees, saying, "Depart from me, for I am a sinful man, O Lord." [9] For he and all who were with him were astonished at the catch of fish that they had taken, [10] and so also were James and John, sons of Zebedee, who were partners with Simon. And Jesus said to Simon, "Do not be afraid; from now on you will be catching men."

The two stories are told very differently, but taken together, they give a fuller picture of what happened. Jesus gave his sermon on the boat, then performed the miraculous catch. When Peter's nets could not hold the fish, Peter signaled to his partners, James and John, who assisted in pulling the fish in. This miracle complete, Jesus has his conversation, calling Peter to discipleship. He then heads down the shoreline where James and John are mending the nets damaged by the enormous haul of fish and calls them as well.

Not only does this explain Matthew's account of them mending their nets, it also explains why they were so willing to leave everything and follow him after having witnessed the miracle.

How did Herod hear of Jesus?

Matthew 14:1-2
English Standard Version (ESV)

The Death of John the Baptist

14 At that time Herod the tetrarch heard about the fame of Jesus, ² and he said to his servants, "This is John the Baptist. He has been raised from the dead; that is why these miraculous powers are at work in him."

Luke 8:1-3
English Standard Version (ESV)

Women Accompanying Jesus

8 Soon afterward he went on through cities and villages, proclaiming and bringing the good news of the kingdom of God. And the twelve were with him, ² and also some women who had been healed of evil spirits and infirmities: Mary, called Magdalene, from whom seven demons had gone out, ³ *and Joanna, the wife of Chuza, Herod's household manager*, and Susanna, and many others, who provided for them out of their means.

Luke mentions in passing that the wife of Herod's household manager was one of the women who followed and supported Jesus. This seemingly random fact explains why Herod seems to be so informed and interested in Jesus' ministry throughout the Gospels.

The Mockery of Jesus

Matthew 26:66-68
English Standard Version (ESV)

[66] What is your judgment?" They answered, "He deserves death." [67] Then they spit in his face and struck him. And some slapped him, [68] saying, "Prophesy to us, you Christ! Who is it that struck you?"

Luke 22:63-65
English Standard Version (ESV)

Jesus Is Mocked

[63] Now the men who were holding Jesus in custody were mocking him as they beat him. [64] They also blindfolded him and kept asking him, "Prophesy! Who is it that struck you?" [65] And they said many other things against him, blaspheming him.

After Jesus was found guilty by the Jewish council, they humiliated him. While this mockery and abuse is recorded in both Matthew and Luke, Matthew leaves out a critical detail. Why would they ask him to prophecy who hit him? Luke tells us the reason: they blindfolded him before they hit him. If Matthew was the only gospel available, we would be left to guess.

Peter at the entrance

Matthew 26:71
English Standard Version (ESV)

⁷¹ And when he went out to the entrance, another servant girl saw him, and she said to the bystanders, "This man was with Jesus of Nazareth."

Matthew doesn't explain to us how it is that Peter made it into the entrance of the hall. We just find him there in a restricted area where he, a follower of the man on trial, would not have been welcome. Happily, John clears this up for us:

John 18:15-17
English Standard Version (ESV)

Peter Denies Jesus

¹⁵ Simon Peter followed Jesus, and so did another disciple. Since that disciple was known to the high priest, he entered with Jesus into the courtyard of the high priest, ¹⁶ but Peter stood outside at the door. So the other disciple, who was known to the high priest, went out and spoke to the servant girl who kept watch at the door, and brought Peter in. ¹⁷ The servant girl at the door said to Peter, "You also are not one of this man's disciples, are you?" He said, "I am not."

John tells us that "another disciple" (probably John himself) was known to the High Priest and used his influence to gain entrance for Peter.

The feeding of the five thousand

Mark 6:30-39
English Standard Version (ESV)

Jesus Feeds the Five Thousand

[30] The apostles returned to Jesus and told him all that they had done and taught. [31] And he said to them, "Come away by yourselves to a desolate place and rest a while." For many were coming and going, and they had no leisure even to eat. [32] And they went away in the boat to a desolate place by themselves. [33] Now many saw them going and recognized them, and they ran there on foot from all the towns and got there ahead of them. [34] When he went ashore he saw a great crowd, and he had compassion on them, because they were like sheep without a shepherd. And he began to teach them many things. [35] And when it grew late, his disciples came to him and said, "This is a desolate place, and the hour is now late. [36] Send them away to go into the surrounding countryside and villages and buy themselves something to eat." [37] But he answered them, "You give them something to eat." And they said to him, "Shall we go and buy two hundred denarii worth of bread and give it to them to eat?" [38] And he said to them, "How many loaves do you have? Go and see." And when they had found out, they said, "Five, and two fish." [39] Then he commanded them all to sit down in groups on the green grass.

John 6:1-10
English Standard Version (ESV)

Jesus Feeds the Five Thousand

6 After this Jesus went away to the other side of the Sea of Galilee, which is the Sea of Tiberias. ²And a large crowd was following him, because they saw the signs that he was doing on the sick. ³Jesus went up on the mountain, and there he sat down with his disciples. ⁴Now the Passover, the feast of the Jews, was at hand. ⁵Lifting up his eyes, then, and seeing that a large crowd was coming toward him, Jesus said to Philip, "Where are we to buy bread, so that these people may eat?" ⁶He said this to test him, for he himself knew what he would do. ⁷Philip answered him, "Two hundred denarii worth of bread would not be enough for each of them to get a little." ⁸One of his disciples, Andrew, Simon Peter's brother, said to him, ⁹"There is a boy here who has five barley loaves and two fish, but what are they for so many?" ¹⁰Jesus said, "Have the people sit down." Now there was much grass in the place. So the men sat down, about five thousand in number.

There are several things to take note of in these parallel passages. The first is that Mark's account tells us that "many were coming and going and they had no leisure even to eat." What would account for so much foot traffic through the otherwise modest region of Capernaum? Well, John tells us in his account: the Passover was at hand.

This is collaborated by the casual mention Mark makes that "He commanded them all to sit down in groups *on the green grass.*" In the Middle East, and especially in the region of Capernaum, it is very arid, and there is a very specific time of year (about a month and a half) during which the grass is green. This time of year lines up with the Passover season.

An even more fascinating point in this narrative is that Jesus turns to Philip and asks "Where are we to buy bread, so that these people may eat?"

While John explains to us that this question was a test leading up to a miracle, it is still peculiar which disciple Jesus chose to ask this to. Why such an obscure disciple as Philip?

In Luke's account of this same miracle, we discover where the miracle took place: "On their return the apostles told him all that they had done. And he took them and withdrew apart to a town called Bethsaida." (Luke 9:10)

How does this relate to Philip? Well, in the first chapter of John, we discover that "Now Philip was from Bethsaida...." (John 1:44)

To summarize, Luke tells us that the miracle occurs in Bethsaida, while John tells us that Jesus asked Philip where to find food, and elsewhere, that Philip was from Bethsaida. Only by comparing these two gospels do we get a fuller picture about what, exactly, is going on.

Traveling through Samaria

In Luke 9:53, Jesus is turned away from the country of Samaria because he is headed to Jerusalem to celebrate Passover.

This passage becomes much more meaningful when viewed in light of the record of Jesus's other trip through Samaria recorded in John chapter 4. On this event, Jesus was coming *from* Judea rather than going through it. The motivation for Samaritans rejecting Jewish pilgrims going to celebrate Passover at the temple in Jerusalem becomes perfectly clear, in Jesus' conversation with the woman at the well. Jesus mentions the fact that there is a disagreement between Samaritans and Jews regarding where the faithful should worship. This disagreement leads to Samaritans being hostile to pilgrims headed to Jerusalem.

We also know, from this passage, that there were still four months until the harvest season during which Passover was held, as Jesus remarks to his disciples: "Do you not say, 'There are yet four months, then comes the harvest'? Look, I tell you, lift up your eyes, and see that the fields are white for harvest."(John 4:35)

Since they were headed away from Judea, and the Passover was four months off, the Samaritans were unlikely to be hostile.

Jesus Walks on Water

The book of John gives this account of Jesus walking on water:

John 6:16-25
English Standard Version (ESV)

Jesus Walks on Water

[16] When evening came, his disciples went down to the sea, [17] got into a boat, and started across the sea to Capernaum. It was now dark, and *Jesus had not yet come to them.* [18] The sea became rough *because a strong wind was blowing.* [19] When they had rowed about three or four miles, they saw Jesus walking on the sea and coming near the boat, and they were frightened. [20] But he said to them, "It is I; do not be afraid." [21] Then they were glad to take him into the boat, and immediately the boat was at the land to which they were going. [22] On the next day *the crowd that remained on the other side of the sea saw that there had been only one boat there, and that Jesus had not entered the boat with his disciples, but that his disciples had gone away alone.* [23] *Other boats from*

Tiberias came near the place where they had eaten the bread after the Lord had given thanks. ²⁴ So when the crowd saw that Jesus was not there, nor his disciples, they themselves got into the boats and went to Capernaum, seeking Jesus.

²⁵ When they found him on the other side of the sea, they said to him, "Rabbi, when did you come here?"

There are several details to be gleaned from here. Firstly, the people following Jesus saw the disciples leave without Jesus; therefore, they thought Jesus was still with them. When they could not find Jesus, they were confused because no other boats had left port, although a few had come from Tiberias.

Question: If there was a large storm, why had boats come from Tiberias even though none had left that port?

The answer comes to us from Matthew's account of the same event:

Matthew 14:22-24
English Standard Version (ESV)

²² Immediately he made the disciples get into the boat and go before him to the other side, while he dismissed the crowds. ²³ And after he had dismissed the crowds, he went up on the mountain by himself to pray. When evening came, he was there alone, ²⁴ but the boat by this time was a long way from the land, beaten by the waves, for the wind was against them.

This passage tells us that the storm winds were blowing in the opposite direction of where they were traveling, Capernaum. Tiberias is on the same side of the sea as Capernaum, so the boats coming from Tiberias had the wind at their backs, making such a trip possible.

These are just some examples of undesigned coincidences wherein the various Gospels unintentionally support one another's account in a way that is consistent with eyewitness testimony. Author JJ Blunt and others have documented hundreds such instances.

By providing such casual and unintentional support of one another, the Gospels begin to look remarkably like the kinds of eyewitness testimonies that historians – and for that matter, police – look for to verify the truth of an account.

Part III
THE TRANSMISSION OF THE DOCUMENTS

Chapter 12
THE CRITICISM

Even assuming that the original New Testament documents were early, accurate, eyewitness accounts, what assurance do we have that the copies we have 2000 years later are in any sense accurate?

It is a popular notion among laymen and scholars that the New Testament documents were intentionally chosen to conveniently serve the purposes of the church. Even those who do not buy into the more conspiratorial theories will often say that there is no way that - through the process of copying and recopying the manuscripts - the version of the Bible we now have is very accurate.

How were the documents that form our current New Testament chosen, and were they transmitted accurately or not?

Bible Scholar Bart Ehrman nicely sums up the argument against Biblical accuracy in this quote from his book *Jesus, Interrupted: Revealing the Hidden Contradictions in the Bible {and Why We Don't Know About Them}:*[41]

One of the most amazing and perplexing features of mainstream Christianity is that seminarians who learn the historical-critical method in their Bible classes appear to forget all about it when it comes time for them to be pastors. They are taught critical approaches to Scripture, they learn about the discrepancies and contradictions, they discover all sorts of historical errors and mistakes, they come to realize that it is difficult to know whether Moses existed or what Jesus actually said and did, they find that there are other books that were at one time considered canonical but that ultimately did not become part of Scripture (for example, other Gospels and Apocalypses), they come to recognize that a good number of the books of the Bible are pseudonymous (for example, written in the name of an apostle by someone else), that in fact we don't have the original copies of any of the biblical books but only copies made centuries later, all of which have been altered. They learn all of this, and yet when they enter church ministry they appear to put it back on the shelf.

Here, Ehrman makes the following claims:

- The Bible contains historical errors and mistakes
- It is difficult to know what Jesus actually said and did
- Many of the Biblical books were written under pseudonyms (not by the traditionally ascribed author)
- The canon of scripture has been in flux and is in some ways arbitrary
- The original texts don't survive and the copies are hundreds of years removed from the originals
- All of the copies have been altered from the original texts
- The Bible contains a variety of discrepancies and contradictions

For the purposes of external apologetics, we are only seeking to defend that the information we have regarding Jesus's life and the actions and beliefs of his followers that stemmed from his life are accurate enough that the basic tenets of Christianity (salvation of sin through faith in Christ's death and resurrection) can be shown to be correct.

In the course of our study so far, we have addressed Erhman's assertion that the Bible contains historical errors and mistakes, that it is difficult to know what Jesus actually said and did, and that the authors of the Gospels were not who tradition claims they were.

In this section, we will attempt to defend against the claims that the canon of scripture was arbitrary, and that the scripture has been significantly altered over hundreds of years of copying and recopying. While our entire study has touched over and again on the idea that there are a variety of contradictions within scripture, this claim is so broad that it would be impossible to address all of these supposed contradictions in this text. But first, a note related to internal apologetics.

There are two extreme approaches to the biblical texts. On one extreme is total skepticism. This characterizes the approach that Bart Ehrman has adopted. Essentially, total skepticism clings to the premise that little or nothing can be known about the original texts, and the history they purport to follow is either patently false or corrupted beyond recognition. This approach assumes that the Christian faith is a fabrication and interprets every piece of evidence from this assumption.

On the other extreme is absolute certainty. This approach assumes that every aspect of the original text has been preserved to the letter, and that all Christian ideals and doctrines are unquestionable.

Total skepticism, as we will see, is unwarranted and turns a blind eye to the mountains of evidence that shows there is very good reason to rely on the texts as accurate portrayals of what the original authors wrote and witnessed.

Absolute certainty is a naive and very dangerous position to take, and has ultimately ended up disillusioning and turning away many Christians from their faith when some evidence arises that puts something they have believed into question. Absolute certainty, also known as dogmatism, tends to sit like a house of cards, such that if one belief collapses, the entire system collapses.

There are, in fact, a variety of errors that have crept into the text over the millennium, as we will show. That said, there is very, very good evidence that the essential truths of scripture have remained true and accurate, and by comparing the hundreds of manuscripts we now have, these errors are fairly easy to spot and correct. God has used human scribes and scholars to transmit the texts down to us. Humans are prone to mistakes, but God's truth remains. This is the claim we will attempt to defend in the following chapters.

When a pastor opens his Bible on Sunday, and all of the people in the pews open theirs, the words that the pastor reads usually differ somewhat from what each parishioner reads. Various Christians use various translations, and each conveys the meaning of the text in different wording.

This fact does not appear to bother many Christians. They take it as given that the truth of scripture is conveyed, despite the differences in translation.

This same attitude may best characterize the position many Christian scholars take about the variations in the copies of scripture over the years. They acknowledge that not every copy is identical to the next, but they also are able to see that the essential truth has been preserved.

Chapter 13
FORMATION OF THE
NEW TESTAMENT CANON

In *The Da Vinci Code* (2009), author Dan Brown popularized the notion that the canon of scripture and the doctrines of the Christian church were not actually established until the first council of Nicaea (CE 325). He and others like him believe that Constantine took a variety of documents from various cultic groups and assembled them into a book, and that this council was the first place in which they invented the claim that Jesus was God incarnate. This established a made-up religion for the purpose of controlling the masses.

The twenty-seven books that form the New Testament also happen to be the earliest Christian writings still in existence. We know from references in the epistles that there were more letters in circulation in the early church than just the ones we have in existence. We also know that documents from the first century that were faithfully copied and passed down such that we still have copies available today are very few and far between.

The fact that these twenty-seven documents were important enough that they were copiously recopied, passed around, translated into other languages, and preserved while others were not is a strong indication that, very early on, the church recognized these documents as definitive.

While Ehrman and his ilk would contend that at least some of the New Testament books were written by other than the traditionally ascribed author, we know from this study that they all have an arguably firsthand connection to apostolic sources. They were either written by direct apostles of Christ (Jesus' disciples and Paul), by brothers of Jesus (James and Jude), or by those who were recording the direct eyewitness accounts of the apostles (Mark and Luke).

Throughout the New Testament, the authors confirm one another as scriptural. Luke copies whole passages from Matthew and Mark. Peter, in his second epistles, confirms Paul's teachings as scripture:

2 Peter 3:15-16
English Standard Version (ESV)

[15] And count the patience of our Lord as salvation, just as our beloved brother Paul also wrote to you according to the wisdom given him, [16] as he does in all his letters when he speaks in them of these matters. There are some things in them that are hard to understand, which the ignorant and unstable twist to their own destruction, as they do the other Scriptures.

It is important to note from this passage that Peter refers to more than one writing of Paul's, indicating a collection of works of some type. More than this, however, it is significant that Peter *assumes* his audience was aware of these writings. Peter's statement seems to indicate that his audience already accepted these writings as scriptural in nature.

As discussed earlier in this book, Paul quotes Luke's gospel as scripture. In 1 Timothy 5:17-18, Paul quotes Luke 10:7 and refers to it as "scripture." In 1 Corinthians 11:23-25, Paul says, "For I received from the Lord what I also delivered to you," and then goes on to quote Luke 22:19-20. Note that Paul introduces his quotation as "from the Lord." Once again, the passages assume that the audience is familiar with and accepts the scriptural authority of the cited text.

Thus, the New Testament support for each other's documents goes something like this:

Peter → Paul → Luke → Matthew and Mark

This alone indicates the majority of the New Testament documents, including three of the four gospels, Acts, and all of Paul's epistles.

This is contemporary evidence that, in the very decades they were written, these books were immediately recognized for their doctrinal significance and placed on par with the books of the Old Testament in terms of authority.

"The Church Fathers Period," is detailed by writings of the direct successors to the apostles. In his book, *Our Legacy* (2001), Dr. John Hannah says that during the "Church Father" period, there was general agreement on doctrines[45]. While they cited as many as nineteen out of the twenty-seven currently accepted New Testament books in the available writings of the time period, they lived in an age of vast illiteracy, and so the oral tradition was held as equally authoritative to scripture.

The next period of the Church that Hannah describes he calls the age of "The Apologists.[46]" During this time, overt hostility toward Christianity from the culture and governing powers was on the rise. Worse, disagreements and challenges were coming from within the Church itself.

These challenges forced the Church leaders of the time to have to define what their source of authority was so that they could address the many conflicting opinions regarding doctrine and beliefs. In defining their authority, the oral tradition became marginalized largely because the Gnostic sect was claiming a different oral tradition to support their views. Church Fathers began to look to the writings of the apostles as alone being authoritative, and the idea of a canon of scripture began to emerge.

The apocryphal documents that might possibly have competed for a spot in the canon did not appear on the scene until the late second century[47]. Once again, it is more than just coincidence that the earliest documents were accepted and the later documents were rejected.

The canons of the day varied. The entire Old Testament and all twenty-seven books of the currently accepted New Testament were held as sacred in one or another of the churches, but few, if any, had access to all of them[46].

While the Gospels and all of Paul's epistles were accepted universally, there was some dispute over a few books like Jude and Hebrews[46]. However, even if all of the books that were disputed at the time were removed, the core doctrines of the Gospel are still affirmed by the remaining. This, then, cannot be regarded as a change made to scriptures in order to advance an agenda.

In the course of this book, we have repeatedly referenced the Muratorian Fragment, a document that lists and provides an introduction to a number of New Testament documents. While the earliest copy we currently possess of the fragment is from the seventh or eighth century, the original can be dated as early as 180CE, hundreds of years before the first council of Nicaea. This fragment lists twenty-two of the twenty-seven New Testament books (the four Gospels, Acts, all thirteen epistles of Paul, Jude, 1 John, 2 John, arguably Third John, and Revelation)[48].

In his article on early Christian writings, Michael Kruger (2013) states that early Christians *did* frequently reference noncanonical works, but stresses that, as a whole, they did not reference them as scriptural or authoritative—merely helpful or illuminating[49]. This is a fact that is frequently glossed over by skeptics who use the noncanonical references of early Christians as an incriminating fact to break down the legitimacy of the canon.

As to the claim that the canon was formed by Constantine at the first council of Nicaea, the council of Nicaea had nothing to do with deciding a canon. The Nicaean Council was called to address a spreading heresy that called into question the equality of Christ to God. At this council, the leaders in attendance hammered out a common understanding of Jesus' nature, leading to the Nicaean Creed[50].

The canon of scripture was never actually determined in an official capacity. At best, it was increasingly *recognized* by churches for having been what it always was. In many ways, the formation of the canon was never officiated by any human or group of people. It just happened.

Even Bart Ehrman admits this when he says:

> The canon of the New Testament was ratified by widespread consensus rather than by official proclamation. (Ehrman, Lost Christianities (2005), p. 231)

As seen here, even critics will admit that the canon seems to have fallen into place naturally. However, even if the contested books were removed entirely, the essentials of Christian doctrine remain very much intact, giving no credence to the claim that the current version of Christianity was invented in the fourth century.

Chapter 14
Transmission of the New Testament Documents

It is worth noting that the harmony and overall message of the New Testament is such that it would have to have been heavily rewritten—or fabricated by a common source—in order to cast doubt on the essential message of the gospel, that message being: salvation from sin through repentance and faith in Christ.

That said, there is extensive evidence that the truth of the New Testament has been preserved and transmitted with extraordinary accuracy.

Copies of the Greek Manuscripts

We have more than 5,600 copies of the New Testament manuscripts in the original Greek language, with more being recovered all the time. Within the last nine years, seventy more have been recovered. Many more are being recovered in recent times in old Soviet Bloc countries to which scholars are only recently gaining access. As of current, the earliest New Testament fragments available are dated between 90 and 150CE. There are over 100 copies of New Testament documents in our possession dated from the fourth century or before[51].

To put this in context, we have exactly four manuscripts of the biography of Alexander the Great (our primary source of information about his life), the earliest of which is dated 1200CE. The other three are from 1500CE and are based on the one from 1200[51].

There are five Roman historians without which we would know practically nothing of Roman history. These include Herodotus (c. 484-425BCE), Thucydides (c. 460-395BCE), Livy (c.59BCE-17CE), Tacitus (c. 56-117CE), and Suetonius (c. 69-122CE). The oldest manuscripts of these five authors come 300 years after the originals. We have fewer than 400 manuscripts of these authors. For Thucydides, the earliest manuscript we have is dated 500 years after the original, and then only as fragmentary copies. For Livy, there are only twenty-seven surviving manuscripts, the earliest dating from the fourth century. For Tacitus, there are only three surviving manuscripts dating 800 years after the original[51].

The average classical author has less than twenty copies of their work still in existence. There is one thousand times more material on the New Testament than on any classical author[51].

Other ancient manuscripts have holes or are missing pages, and scholars have to fill in the blanks based on conjecture. We have so many copies of the New Testament manuscripts that there are no holes at all in our knowledge of the text.

This means that the New Testament is the most verifiable ancient document in history. Despite this, the works of the classical authors are almost never questioned for their authenticity, whereas the New Testament documents are ruthlessly attacked, displaying a staggering double-standard.

For the New Testament, the first copies we have are decades after the originals, not centuries. We have over 5,600 Greek copies, 5,000 in Latin, 5 to 10 thousand in other languages, over a million quotations in the church fathers[51].

The Importance of Translation

When an early document like the New Testament is translated into a new language, it provides an invaluable resource to interpreters. The early translators had to preserve the meaning of the original documents in the act of translation.

Think of a translation as a snapshot of what the text looked like at the time it was copied. Once the Greek manuscript of, say, 200CE is translated into Latin, every Latin copy thereafter is not retranslated from the latest Greek manuscript. Rather, the Latin copies are recopied off one another.

In 1604, translators began to translate the New Testament using three of the best Greek manuscripts available at the time. The King James Version of the Bible is an accurate reflection of scholars' understanding of the available manuscripts of that time period. In 1989, the New Revised Standard Version of the Bible was published. This version reflected the most recent manuscript evidence and translation updates. The NRSV is a more accurate reflection of the original Greek manuscripts because more and earlier documents were used in the translation process. Each of these translations is a snapshot of scholarly understanding of the original documents at the time period.

Early on, the New Testament was translated from Greek into Latin, and these Latin translations swept across the Middle East and Europe as it became the primary language. We now have over 10,000 manuscripts in Latin[51].

The New Testament was also translated from Greek into dozens of other languages; together, we have about 5,000 of these other translations[51].

By comparing the earliest translations to the original Greek documents, it is easy to see how accurate our current versions are based on how closely the meaning preserved in the translations match the originals.

The Early Church Fathers

The *early church fathers* wrote superfluous commentaries and essays on doctrine and scripture, quoting extensively from the Greek documents. If we had *no* copies of the documents, virtually the entire New Testament could be reconstructed multiple times over by taking the quotations from the *early church fathers*. There are more than 1 million quotations from the New Testament from these early church fathers[51].

Once again, these can be compared with the copies of the text in order to verify their accuracy.

Translation Variants

When he makes his case against the accuracy of the transmission of the New Testament, Bart Ehrman cites several facts that seem to build a convincing case that the New Testament we now hold is very different from the original document it was based on.

The Greek New Testament has 138,162 words. Taken together, all of the copies of the New Testament documents that we possess contain roughly 400,000 variants (differences in spelling, sentence structure, texts inserted or missing). Ehrman and others like him use a statistic like this to point out that there are more variants than there are words in the Greek New Testament[51].

The reason we have a lot of variants is because we have a lot of manuscripts, as shown above. What Ehrman and others tend to underemphasize is how many of these "variants" involve misspellings and word order, things that are easily corrected by comparing the many available copies.

More significant variants have been recognized early in the translation process and are all footnoted in modern Bibles. Possibly the three most significant variations are these:

The Long Ending of Mark's Gospel

Mark 16:9-20
English Standard Version (ESV)

[Some of the earliest manuscripts do not include 16:9–20.]

Jesus Appears to Mary Magdalene

⁹ [[Now when he rose early on the first day of the week, he appeared first to Mary Magdalene, from whom he had cast out seven demons. ¹⁰ She went and told those who had been with him, as they mourned and wept. ¹¹ But when they heard that he was alive and had been seen by her, they would not believe it.

Jesus Appears to Two Disciples

¹² After these things he appeared in another form to two of them, as they were walking into the country. ¹³ And they went back and told the rest, but they did not believe them.

The Great Commission

¹⁴ Afterward he appeared to the eleven themselves as they were reclining at table, and he rebuked them for their unbelief and hardness of heart, because they had not believed those who saw him after he had risen. ¹⁵ And he said to them, "Go into all the world and proclaim the gospel to the whole creation. ¹⁶ Whoever believes and is baptized will be saved, but whoever does not believe will be condemned. ¹⁷ And these signs will accompany those who believe: in my name they will cast out demons; they will speak

in new tongues; [18] they will pick up serpents with their hands; and if they drink any deadly poison, it will not hurt them; they will lay their hands on the sick, and they will recover."

[19] So then the Lord Jesus, after he had spoken to them, was taken up into heaven and sat down at the right hand of God. [20] And they went out and preached everywhere, while the Lord worked with them and confirmed the message by accompanying signs.]]

Mark 16:9-20, called the "Long ending" to *Mark*, is a passage not contained in the earliest and most reliable Greek manuscripts. While it *is* contained in the *majority* of the available Greek manuscripts, it appears to have been an early addition, not part of the original text[52].

The transition between verse 8 and 9 in Mark 16 is abrupt and awkward, and 9-20 use Greek words that Mark uses nowhere else in his gospel. Moreover, there is the reference to Jesus casting out seven demons from Mary Magdalene, which seems odd to bring up only now in the narrative. The whole section reads as if it had been tagged on to the text by someone other than Mark.

Since without these verses the *Gospel of Mark* ends quite abruptly, scholars tend to believe that this is an early effort to place a more complete ending to *Mark* using information derived from the other Gospels and early traditions about Jesus' resurrection[52].

What is significant about this artifact is that it has been long recognized by scribes and scholars. Even in the earliest Greek manuscripts that include this passage, there are scribal notes indicating to the reader that this passage is not part of the original text, such that, almost from the beginning, Christians have known about this addition.

The Woman caught in Adultery

John 7:53-8:11
English Standard Version (ESV)

[The earliest manuscripts do not include 7:53–8:11.]

The Woman Caught in Adultery

[53] [[They went each to his own house, 8 [1] but Jesus went to the Mount of Olives. [2] Early in the morning he came again to the temple. All the people came to him, and he sat down and taught them. [3] The scribes and the Pharisees brought a woman who had been caught in adultery, and placing her in the midst [4] they said to him, "Teacher, this woman has been caught in the act of adultery. [5] Now in the Law Moses commanded us to stone such women. So what do you say?" [6] This they said to test him, that they might have some charge to bring against him. Jesus bent down and wrote with his finger on the ground. [7] And as they continued to ask him, he stood up and said to them, "Let him who is without sin among you be the first to throw a stone at her." [8] And once more he bent down and wrote on the ground. [9] But when they heard it, they went away one by one, beginning with the older ones, and Jesus was left alone with the woman standing before him. [10] Jesus stood up and said to her, "Woman, where are they? Has no one condemned you?" [11] She said, "No one, Lord." And Jesus said, "Neither do I condemn you; go, and from now on sin no more."]]

This story does not appear in the New Testament documents until Codex Bezae (D), dated from the fifth century.

This particular document is highly eccentric and has a variety of unusual variations[53].

Scholars note that this story interrupts the flow of the narrative and features language not typical of John's style (some have noted that it seems more typical of Luke's language)[54].

When surveying the large number of manuscripts available, this story tends to wander throughout the manuscripts. Many do not contain this story at all. Some place it after verse 36, 44, 52, or 21:25. One manuscript actually places it in the Gospel of Luke, after Luke 21:38[54].

It is worth noting that a number of the early manuscripts that *include* this passage also include scribal notes indicating doubt about its inclusion. This is significant, because it shows that even ancient Christian scholars were aware of its dubious nature. None of the scriptural commentaries written by early church fathers even mention this passage until the twelfth century[54].

There are a variety of respected Christian scholars who argue from a number of facts that this story may still represent an actual event that happened during the life of Christ and circulated in the church orally or through some written source, before it found its way into copies of John's gospels. They argue this based on the language of the text and from early document evidence[54].

However, legitimate or not, this passage has long been recognized as a spurious addition and not part of the original text, so that its inclusion in the modern Bible is hardly enough to call into question the reliability of the entire text.

There are three that bear witness

The King James Version of 1st John 5:7 reads:

"For there are three that bear record in heaven, the Father, the Word, and the Holy Ghost: and these three are one."

In the ESV, it reads:

"For there are three that testify:"

The longer version in the KJV (and several other English translations) represents a reading found in only eight late manuscripts, four of which contain these words in a marginal note. Most scholars agree that these words found their way into the text as some scribe's notes, inserted in the text, drawing a parallel between John's message and a Trinitarian understanding[55].

The King James and several other translations have preserved these words primarily out of the motivation that they represent possibly the clearest text about God's triune nature.

As with the other artifacts mentioned above, the dubious nature of this passage has been well known for generations.

What we can conclude from examining these three passages is this: Firstly, these relatively large textual variations are extremely rare overall, these three representing the total amount of textual variations that are not mere grammar, word order, and spelling mistakes.

Secondly, these variations are and have been known about by Bible scholars almost from the time they began to appear in the texts, with scribal notes being found alongside all three noting that they probably weren't part of the original.

The final point to emphasize is that none of these passages have any significant impact on Christian doctrine. Their inclusion in the text does no ultimate damage to the scriptural testimony of Jesus's life and work.

What this shows is that humans make mistakes, but that God preserves his truth regardless.

Part IV
HISTORICAL EVIDENCE

Chapter 15
EXTERNAL SUPPORT FOR THE GOSPELS/JESUS

U sing the Bible and the writings of early Christians will only win you so much traction in arguing your case to a skeptic. Why should they believe what any Christian has to say, early or not, when Christianity is the point they're contesting?

One effective answer to this question is that these people were Christians because *they were convinced* by the evidence.

However, if arguments purely based on the Biblical documents and accounts fail to convince, there are *other* evidences. There is significant historical support external to Christian writings that verify the New Testament accounts.

Archeology

Use of Names

Archeology digs have revealed a lot about the first century culture in which the events of the New Testament took place. The most prolific findings archeology has provided concern graves and their inscriptions. Based on these inscriptions, historians can form a fairly accurate picture of the given names popular in that time period from various cultures and regions. Scholar Tal Ilan has been instrumental in forming a catalogue of names that were popular at particular times and in particular regions during the first century based not just on graves, but also on historical documents from the time period. Below is a comparison of the popular names as first century documents and inscriptions confirm and the most frequently used names in New Testament literature[56]:

Popularity of First Century Palestinian Names found in Literature and Archeology:	Popularity of First Century Palestinian Names found in the New Testament:
49.7 percent of the women had one of the nine most popular names	**61.1 percent** of the women had one of the nine most popular names
41.5 percent of the men had one of the nine most popular names	**40.3 percent** of the men had one of the nine most popular names
28.6 percent of the women had the name Mary or Salome	**38.9 percent** of the women had the name Mary or Salome
15.6 percent of the men had the name Simon or Joseph	**18.2 percent** of the men had the name Simon or Joseph
9.6 percent of the women had a name that no one else had	**2.5 percent** of the women had a name that no one else had
7.9 percent of the men had a name that no one else had	**3.9 percent** of the men had a name no one else had

This kind of meticulous and incidental information would be close to impossible to fake if the authors had not been present during the time period about which they were writing or had access to firsthand accounts.

Corroboration from Contemporary Non-Christian Documents

The amount of literature from the first century that survives to this day is tragically small. However, from copies and references in historical material, it is possible to verify a number of facts that support the historicity of Christ and Christians.

Josephus (37-100CE)

Josephus was a Jewish historian writing to a Roman audience. He was a meticulous scholar with a flair for the dramatic. Every indication within Josephus's writings suggests that he was a faithful Jew with no particular sympathy for the Christians.

Josephus refers to Christians several times in his most famous work, *Antiquities of the Jews*. Unfortunately, many of the copies of *Antiquities* that have survived were apparently copied by Christian scribes, and their references to Christ and Christianity appear to have been altered in a well-meaning effort to sanctify them. This has cast suspicion on the authenticity of these references. Below is a quote from one of the earlier translations of Josephus's work that appears to have escaped tampering:

> *At this time there was a wise man who was called Jesus. His conduct was good, and [he] was known to be virtuous. And many people from among the Jews and the other nations became his disciples. Pilate condemned him to be crucified and to die. And those who had become his disciples did not abandon his discipleship. They reported that he had appeared to them three days after his crucifixion and that he was alive; accordingly, he was perhaps the Messiah concerning whom the prophets have recounted wonders.[57]*

This account gives external support that Jesus was an actual, historical figure, that he was considered wise and achieved a following of both Jewish and non-Jewish people. It confirms that he was crucified and that he was reported risen, and that his disciples did not abandon him after his death. These are all important facts to build the case for Christ, as will be seen later.

Sextus Julius Africanus (160-240CE) and the Darkness at Jesus's Crucifixion

Thallus (5-60CE), a Samaritan historian, wrote his three-volume work on the history of the Mediterranean region around the middle of the first century. His work is mostly lost, but Roman historian Sextus Julius Africanus quoted some of Thallus's text in his 221CE *History of the World.*

In one significant quotation, Africanus offers a commentary on Thallus's reference to the unnatural darkness that occurred at Jesus' crucifixion:

> *On the whole world there pressed a most fearful darkness; and the rocks were rent by an earthquake, and many places in Judea and other districts were thrown down. This darkness Thallus, in the third book of his History, calls, as it appears to me without reason, an eclipse of the sun.*[58]

The fact that a Samaritan historian would corroborate one of the more supernatural events associated with Jesus' death (even though denying its supernatural nature) is of invaluable importance, apologetically. Critics could argue that Thallus was taking an unsubstantiated Christian story (which there should be eyewitnesses still around to confirm or refute the story) and trying to give it a natural explanation. In which case, why bother? Or he was referencing a natural event that Christians had used in their myth-building, but this would be easy enough to confirm or deny. Modern astronomical science is advanced enough to tell us if there was an eclipse event in the early first century at that time and place.

Sextus Julius Africanus provided another reference to the darkness at Jesus' crucifixion by citing the 140CE work of history by an author named Phlegon, saying:

> *Phlegon records that, in the time of the Tiberius Ceasar, at full moon, there was a full eclipse of the sun from the sixth hour to the ninth.* [59]

It seems more likely that such darkness actually occurred, and that Thallus and Phlegon are trying to explain it away rather than to accept the Christian explanation.

Tacitus (56-117CE)

Cornelius Tacitus was a high-ranking government official in the Roman Empire, a senator during the reign of Emperor Vespasian and a proconsul of Asia.

In addition to being a powerful politician, he was a prolific historical commentator, writing extensive (and very informative) works on a number of history volumes available at his time period. His surviving writings are well-regarded for their accuracy and information on a number of lost works.

When writing on the notorious fire in Rome during Nero's reign, Tacitus said:

> *Consequently, to get rid of the report, Nero fastened the guilt and inflicted the most exquisite tortures on a class hated for their abominations, called Christians by the populace. Christus, from whom the name had its origin, suffered the extreme penalty during the reign of Tiberius at the hands of one of our procurators, Pontius Pilatus, and a most mischievous superstition, thus checked for the moment, again broke out not only in Judaea, the first source of the evil, but even in Rome, where all things hideous and shameful from every part of the world find their centre and become popular. (Annals, 15:44)*

Clearly in this passage, Tacitus is showing he is no fan of the Christians. But his commentary provides an external confirmation of the early existence and following of Jesus, of his crucifixion as described in the gospels, of the rumor of his resurrection, and the spread of Christian belief to gentiles in the early first century.

Possibly most importantly, Tacitus shows that early Christians were, indeed, persecuted and killed for their beliefs, a powerful argument for the sincerity of this conviction as we will soon see.

By showing his disregard of Christians, Tacitus becomes a hostile witness; a witness whose agenda is NOT intended to benefit the Christian cause, which makes it a more powerful testimony when it provides evidence in favor of Christian claims.

Mara Bar-Serapion (70-Unknown CE)

Mara Bar-Serapion was a Syrian philosopher in the late first century. In a text he wrote to his son, Mara Bar-Serapion included Jesus in a list of influential philosophers who were killed for their teachings:

> *What advantage did the Athenians gain from putting Socrates to death? Famine and plague came upon them as a judgment for their crime. What advantage did the men of Samos gain from burning Pythagoras? In a moment their land was covered with sand. What advantage did the Jews gain from executing their wise King? It was just after that their kingdom was abolished. God justly avenged these three wise men: the Athenians died of hunger; the Samians were overwhelmed by the seas; the Jews, ruined and driven from their land, live in complete dispersion. But Socrates did not die for good; he lived on in the teaching of Plato. Pythagoras did not die for good; he lived on in the statue of Hera. Nor did the wise King die for good; He lived on in the teaching which He had given.[60]*

By now, we have effectively put the nail in the lid of the coffin of the idea that Jesus was just a late legend. At the very least, all of this external testimony is proof positive that Jesus lived, taught provocative concepts, was killed for his teachings, and had devoted followers who doggedly clung to their beliefs and were persecuted as a result.

Mara Bar-Serapion does us the additional favor of connecting the pieces between Jesus' crucifixion and the raid of Jerusalem in 70CE; and as a secular philosopher, he lists Jesus as a wise teacher unworthy of the death he was given.

Phlegon (80-140CE)

Phlegon was a Greek Historian who wrote a number of works in the early second century. His work is referenced above by Sextus Julius Africanus. Much of his work is lost, but Origen, a Christian writer from the early third century, commented on one of his histories:

> *Now Phlegon, in the thirteenth or fourteenth book, I think, of his Chronicles, not only ascribed to Jesus a knowledge of future events (although falling into confusion about some things which refer to Peter, as if they referred to Jesus), but also testified that the result corresponded to his predictions. So that he also, by these very admissions regarding foreknowledge, as if against his will, expressed his opinion that the doctrines taught by the fathers of our system were not devoid of divine power.*

> *And with regard to the eclipse in the time of Tiberius Caesar, in whose reign Jesus appears to have been crucified, and the great earthquakes which then took place, Phlegon too, I think, has written in the thirteenth or fourteenth book of his Chronicles.*

> ***He imagines also that both the earthquake and the darkness were an invention; but regarding these, we have in the preceding pages made our defence [sic], according to our ability, adducing the testimony of Phlegon, who relates***

that these events took place at the time when our Savior suffered.[61]

In this passage, Origen has done all of the apologetic work for us. It is worth mentioning that Plegon was a bit of a sensationalist in his writing, gladly recounting supernatural events connected to Greek and Roman religion and prophets.

What is interesting here is that Phlegon, who otherwise is quick to accept a supernatural explanation, is taking early accounts about the earthquake and eclipse that occurred at the time of Jesus's crucifixion and attempting to assign them a natural explanation. This effort to explain away these events only adds to their probability.

Another thing worth mentioning is that Phlegon is writing around 100 years after the events he is recording. Since he is referencing the eclipse and earthquake that occurred at Jesus's death, it shows that these were not late inventions of the church. If they were inventions, they were early, and the accounts had become so widespread that they had reached Greece by this time. Moreover, Phlegon felt that they were worth explaining away, which shows the influence these events had had on people who knew about them.

The Talmud

The Talmud is an ancient record of the theological discussions held by Jewish Rabbis of the time period. While the Talmud is dated from around the fifth century, some of the discussion recorded therein date back to the first and second century.

The person of Jesus of Nazareth is something of a hot button topic within the Talmud:

"Jesus practiced magic and led Israel astray" (b. Sanhedrin 43a; cf. t. Shabbat 11.15; b. Shabbat 104b).

"Rabbi Hisda (d. 309) said that Rabbi Jeremiah bar Adda said, 'What is that which is written, "No evil will befall you, nor shall any plague come near your house"? (Psalm 91:10)... "No evil will befall you" (means) that evil dreams and evil thoughts will not tempt you; "nor shall any plague come near your house" (means) that you will not have a son or a disciple who burns his food like Jesus of Nazareth'" (b. Sanhedrin 103a; cf. b. Berakhot 17b)

"It was taught: On the day before the Passover they hanged Jesus. A herald went before him for forty days (proclaiming), 'He will be stoned, because he practiced magic and enticed Israel to go astray. Let anyone who knows anything in his favor come forward and plead for him.' But nothing was found in his favor, and they hanged him on the day before the Passover" (b. Sanhedrin 43a).

While these quotes do not directly correlate in every respect with the gospel accounts, they do admit to Jesus' miraculous (or magical) power, his following, and mentions his crucifixion.

It is significant that the majority of these accounts, most of them hostile testimony, at least make passing reference to Jesus' supernatural association, the most challenging fact when discussing the Jesus accounts with a skeptical audience.

Chapter 16
THE MINIMAL FACTS ARGUMENT

Form Criticism

"Form Criticism" is a method of examining ancient documents with a view toward determining something about their origin, authorship, and editing that has occurred over multiple copyings and translations.

Form criticism looks intently at the writing style, themes, and use of language to determine if the text was translated from a previous language, if it had a single or multiple authors, if it has been changed or edited across a number of copyings, if it has been merged or integrated with other texts, etc.

A great deal of what goes on in form criticism is educated speculation. As an example, when applied to the Old Testament book of *Job*, form criticism will take note of the following facts:

- The beginning and end of *Job* appear to be historic or biographical narratives about the person Job, including names of places, numbering of flocks, children, etc.
- The central part of *Job* is highly poetic, unlike the beginning and end

- The character of Elihu appears late in the book, and takes a very different perspective from what Job or his friends have previously taken.

From this, form critics will conclude—among other things—that the book of Job is the merging of at least two separate narratives, one historic and one poetic, and that the character of Elihu was added to the text by a later writer/editor who wanted to insert his or her own philosophy into the book.

Of course, this conclusion trades on the speculation that the original author would be incapable of slipping from one narrative type (historic) into another narrative type (poetic), or that another character arriving late in the conversation would not have been the intent of the original author[s]. It also treats Job as a work of fiction, such that the facts and conversations recorded in the text do not represent anything that ever really happened, which, of course, involves more than a little speculation.

While this type of analysis is a common approach to ancient texts, Christians tend to bulk when this approach is applied to the Bible because they take their beliefs about their religion directly from the Bible and because they believe that God has preserved his truth through the text.

As we have just argued, whether or not one accepts that the New Testament documents were inspired, they are at the very least the most reliable and well-transmitted ancient documents available today.

Whether or not form criticism is warranted in the case of scripture, there *are* some New Testament facts that practically every critic can agree upon.

The Minimal Fact Approach

The Minimal Facts Approach takes a number of facts that are accepted by practically every New Testament scholar, no matter how critical, and from these builds a compelling case for the resurrection of Christ. This approach is significant because the skeptic would have to find an alternative explanation that takes into account every one of these facts without admitting to a supernatural event.

Dr. Gary Habermas spent over five years examining and cataloguing hundreds of prominent secular scholars from the 1980s to current day according to the first-century records that they considered historic facts. The facts listed below are accepted by 75 to 95 percent of New Testament historians according to Dr. Habermas's research[62]:

Jesus was buried in Joseph of Arimathea's tomb

One of the reasons this fact is so universally accepted is that the burial of Jesus can be traced back to the oldest available Christian traditions. In 1 Corinthians 15:3-5, Apostle Paul makes this statement:

1 Corinthians 15:3-5
English Standard Version (ESV)

"For I delivered to you as of first importance what I also received:

that Christ died for our sins in accordance with the Scriptures,

that he was buried,

that he was raised on the third day in accordance with the Scriptures,

and that he appeared to Cephas, then to the twelve.

What Paul is quoting here is generally agreed by the majority of scholars, no matter how liberal, to be a sort of primitive gospel, a "saying" that passed around Christian circles before any New Testament documents were written. This is partially because *1 Corinthians* is thought to be one of the earliest New Testament books ever written, and because this quote reads like a little poem or ditty in the Greek, looking almost like a proverb or a slogan.

Paul's preamble to the "saying," "For I delivered to you ... what I also received" is rabbinical language for passing along some tradition or truth.

Because this "saying" presumably predates any of the New Testament documents and mentions the fact of his death and burial, it makes it a powerful testament for the basic facts of the gospel message.

This is not, however, the only evidence that Jesus' burial is considered part of the oldest Christian material. It is significant that Mark's gospel, which is considered the oldest of the four gospels—and based on even older source material—mentions the burial in its Passion Narrative. Since the Passion Narrative is a consistent feature across the four gospels, this argues the source material agrees on this aspect, and the older the material, the less likely it is to be legendary.

Joseph of Arimathea was mentioned by name as the man responsible for burying Jesus, and in a tomb that he owned. Joseph of Arimathea was also mentioned as a member of the Sanhedrin. This is significant because early Christians would not have made up such a character due to the deep resentment they held toward the Jewish rulers, both for Jesus' condemnation and their ongoing persecution. This argues for him being a real, historic personage.

Not only this, but there is also no evidence of any competing burial stories of Jesus circulating at any time. One would expect, if this was fiction, that there would be at least one story that didn't include a Sanhedrin member as the benefactor.

If Joseph of Arimathea was responsible for Jesus's burial, then the place of his burial would have been widely known. The fact that Jesus's burial place was known to Jews and Romans alike is significant because it means that either party could have easily produced Jesus' body as evidence that he was, indeed, still dead and not resurrected.

The Tomb was empty on the third day

It may seem unlikely that liberal, nonbelieving scholars would admit to this fact, but there are a series of facts that scholars *do* accept that lead inescapably to this conclusion.

As with the burial, the story of the empty tomb can be traced back to the early source material in the book of Mark. The earliest manuscripts of Mark's gospel end with the women discovering an empty tomb. What is truly significant about this is that the best manuscript evidence available on Mark does *not* include the appearance and ascension of the risen Christ, which makes it more palatable to skeptics, but it *does* include the women discovering the empty tomb.

The primitive gospel that Paul quotes in 1 Corinthians 15:3-5 also makes allusion to the empty tomb, such that this correlates the very early sources from which Mark is working.

This story is simple and grounded rather than looking like myth or legend. It has women discovering the empty tomb. Such an account would have been considered worthless as eyewitness testimony at that time period, due to the low respect accorded to women. This paradoxically favors the truthfulness of the account, as anyone trying to make up a convincing story would include male witnesses rather than female ones.

The earliest recorded accusations of the Pharisees were that Jesus' body was stolen, which corroborates the story that the tomb was, indeed, empty. As mentioned before, they could have simply produced the dead body to stop the spread of Christianity once and for all.

A variety of separate people believed they saw a resurrected Jesus

Once again, Paul's list of witnesses from his statement in 1 Corinthians 15:3-5 is a key piece of evidence. Given the early dating of this passage, it would be bold, indeed, to make such a claim if there were, in fact, no eyewitnesses. Paul could be discredited as a fraud very quickly by citing specific witnesses (Cephas/Peter, James, and "the twelve") and by listing numerous witnesses (over 500) that did not exist. And if Paul was discredited, his letters would most likely not continue to be copied and circulated so widely.

The postresurrection appearances of Jesus are not simply reported by one person or group of people on one instance. Rather, it is reported on multiple occasions by multiple people or groups of people, many of which had not communicated with one another prior to witnessing Jesus alive. The reports of the witnesses are not restricted to one or two books, but are independently attested by all four gospels and several of the epistles. Multiple, independent attestation is one of the hallmarks of the truth of an eyewitness statement.

This is something that even the harsh German critic of the resurrection, Gerd L,demann, had to admit to:

> It may be taken as historically certain that Peter and the disciples had experiences after Jesus' death in which Jesus appeared to them as the risen Christ. (Gerd L,demann, What Really Happened to Jesus? trans. John Bowden (Louisville, Kent.: Westminster John Knox Press, 1995), p.80)

The conversion of Jesus' brothers

It is fairly well-documented that James and Jesus' other siblings were skeptics, rejecting their brother rather than embracing him:

John 7:5
English Standard Version (ESV)

⁵ For not even his brothers believed in him.

They tried to keep him from speaking because they doubted his sanity:

Mark 3:20-21
English Standard Version (ESV)

²⁰ Then he went home, and the crowd gathered again, so that they could not even eat. ²¹ And when his family heard it, they went out to seize him, for they were saying, "He is out of his mind."

Jesus, likewise, tended to alienate his nonbelieving siblings in favor of his disciples and followers:

Matthew 12:46-50
English Standard Version (ESV)

Jesus' Mother and Brothers

⁴⁶ While he was still speaking to the people, behold, his mother and his brothers stood outside, asking to speak to him. ⁴⁸ But he replied to the man who told him, "Who is my mother, and who are my brothers?" ⁴⁹ And stretching out his hand toward his disciples, he said, "Here are my mother and my brothers! ⁵⁰ For whoever does the will of my Father in heaven is my brother and sister and mother."

To tell fictitious stories about Jesus' family rejecting him (and vice versa) would have served no obvious purpose, so this much has the ring of truth.

It is significant, then, that Jesus' brothers, Jude and James, were prominent early Christians. James especially after seeing the resurrected Christ (as Paul told us) became a devoted follower to Christ. Moreover, the conversion of Jesus' brothers and sisters was very sudden, happening mere weeks after Jesus's death. By the first chapter of Acts, they were already followers:

Acts 1:14
English Standard Version (ESV)

¹⁴ All these with one accord were devoting themselves to prayer, together with the women and Mary the mother of Jesus, and his brothers.

Formerly dismissive of his brother, James now counted himself as a mere servant:

James 1:1
English Standard Version (ESV)

1 James, a servant of God and of the Lord Jesus Christ,

James became a leader of the church in Jerusalem (Acts 15, Galatians 1:18-19, 2:9) and probably died a martyr's death. Josephus claims that he was stoned (Josephus, *Antiquities of the Jews,* 20:200), and Eusebius cites two sources indicating that James was thrown from the temple, beaten to death with a club (Eusebius, *Ecclesiastical History*, 2.1.5), or a combination of all three (Eusebius, *Ecclesiastical History*, 2.23.11-18) in the late 60s CE.

Testaments like this are important. Some skeptics will assert that claims of early Christian persecution are wildly exaggerated. What is important to note from this is that we have multiple, independent attestations that James, a direct witness to Christ's resurrection, was killed for his beliefs.

Saul's conversion

The most skeptical skeptic cannot deny that Paul was highly influential in penning documents of the New Testament and in framing the theology of the early church. Additionally, study of Paul's reasoning and writing style reveals that his thinking and method of argumentation is consistent with a Pharisaical background. This reinforces the claim in the book of Acts that Paul is a converted Pharisee. In addition to what Acts says, Paul himself claims to have been a Pharisee (Philippians 3:5).

Pharisees were the most vehement opposers and Jewish persecutors of Christians, and Paul confirms what the book of Acts claims about him being a persecutor of the Christian church in the book of Philippians (3:6). Given the independent testimonies of Acts and Philippians of Paul's zealous persecution of Christians and Paul's equally zealous defense of the Christian faith and willingness to be persecuted for his faith as attested by Acts, by his own writing (2 Corinthians 11:23-33), and by church tradition that states that he was imprisoned and martyred in Rome in around 60s CE (Eusebius, *Ecclesiastical History*, 2.25.5), it is all but certain that Paul underwent a sudden and dynamic conversion. The book of Acts claims that Paul's conversion experience was triggered when he witnessed a resurrected Christ, and Paul backs this up in 1 Corinthians 15:8 where he says:

> "Last of all, as to one untimely born, he appeared also to me."

This seems to be strong evidence that Paul believed he had seen a resurrected Christ.

The disciples early belief in a risen Christ was counterintuitive

On the night of Jesus' arrest, the disciples, with the exception of John, fled (Mark 14:50), denied any connection to him (Matthew 26:69-75). Two months later, Peter stood in front of thousands of Jews and boldly accused them of crucifying Jesus and called them to repentance, saying:

> **Acts 2:23-24**
> English Standard Version (ESV)
>
> [23] this Jesus, delivered up according to the definite plan and foreknowledge of God, you crucified and killed by the hands of lawless men. [24] God raised him up, loosing the pangs of death, because it was not possible for him to be held by it.

Shortly thereafter, Peter and the disciples, who had so recently watched their leader killed by Jewish leaders, were arrested and brought before those same Jewish leaders. Peter tells them to their face:

> **Acts 4:10**
> English Standard Version (ESV)
>
> [10] let it be known to all of you and to all the people of Israel that by the name of Jesus Christ of Nazareth, whom you crucified, whom God raised from the dead—by him this man is standing before you well.

Immediately after Jesus' death, the disciples were in a situation where their supposedly messianic leader was violently killed rather than ascending to take David's throne as prophecy had indicated. He was killed by order of the Jewish leaders and by approval of the Roman ones. His larger collection of followers was either dispersed or turncoat, and Jewish *and* Roman factions were stacked against them. They had all abandoned their jobs, families, and lives to follow him, and were now left with nothing.

Under Jewish law, Jesus' manner of execution proved him to be a heretic and under the curse of God (Deuteronomy 21:23), putting them in a position where they had to question everything he had ever taught them.

The Jewish concept of resurrection indicated one, collective resurrection of the dead when the Messiah finally took the throne of Israel, not individual resurrections of single people.

Taking all of these facts into account, it is significant that Jesus' disciples switched from cowardice to boldness seemingly overnight. They not only claimed that Jesus had been resurrected, but gladly suffered torture, disdain, and death for this belief. It seems unlikely, to say the least, that they would have done so for what they knew was a lie.

This fact alone has been a convincing proof for the resurrection.

As Emory University New Testament scholar Luke Johnson puts it:

> *Some sort of powerful, transformative experience is required to generate the sort of movement earliest Christianity was.... (Luke Timothy Johnson, The Real Jesus [San Francisco: Harper San Francisco, 1996], p. 136)*

And the British scholar N. T. Wright sates:

> *That is why, as a historian, I cannot explain the rise of early Christianity unless Jesus rose again, leaving an empty tomb behind him. (N.T. Wright, "The New Unimproved Jesus, Christianity Today [September 13, 1993], p. 26)*

The Existence of the Church

When one does a comparative study of world religions, patterns begin to emerge that help to classify a variety of religions into neat categories. However, classic Christianity—that is, Christianity as it was originally practiced in the first and second centuries, and as it has continued to be practiced by various groups ever since—does not neatly adhere to any of these categories. The Christian Church is an anomaly in the record of world religions. There have historically been several basic types of religions:

State Religions

By far and large, religions have historically been state-established and inseparable from government. Most ancient cultures, including Egypt, Greece, Babylon, Syria, Persia, China, Japan and Rome, required the people to worship the ruler as a god, and integrated the priesthood into the government.

In the late third century—and to some degree ever since—certain countries have instituted various forms of Christianity as state religions. Everyone within England, for instance, was automatically a member of the Anglican Church, regardless of their personal convictions. At various times, the so-called "Christian" church has even tortured and imprisoned people not willing to pledge their allegiance to the Church.

In medieval times, the Church developed a convenient doctrine that basically stated that kings were directly appointed by God, making anyone who chose to defy the monarchy guilty of heresy.

It was this manner of religious despotism that contributed to the colonization and formation of America, as various religious groups, most of them claiming some form of Christianity, fled the enforced religions of Europe.

The idea of separation of church and state, and of freedom of religion, continues to be one of the foundational appeals of the American way.

Religious despotism, however, is a far cry from the Christianity seen in the New Testament. There, people were encouraged to live peaceably and to obey governing authorities, even if those authorities violently disagreed with their religious views. Jesus preached a kingdom that was "not of this world," and commanded his followers to pay their taxes as good citizens.

The Christianity of the Bible is one wherein each person is held personally accountable to God as their authority, and even if they are abused, should not return abuse. The offender, of course, is also personally accountable to God.

Theocracy

While the Jewish government did not elevate the king to the position of God, the Mosaic Law integrated the worship and the law into one system wherein a prophet spoke for God, and the people were responsible for governing themselves.

Later, this was amended so that a king was responsible for enforcing the judicial portion of the Mosaic Law, the priest for maintaining the sacramental part of the law—interceding on behalf of the people for their forgiveness—and the prophets for delivering God's directions to the king and the people in general.

While this system *is* Biblical, it is also intended specifically for the Jewish people. Jesus abolished these laws when he completed his ministry such that to enforce such laws, especially on Gentiles, would be a violation of the Biblical teachings.

Wisdom Religions

Wisdom religions, which are mainly pantheistic in nature, may accrue a wide following over time, as Hinduism and Buddhism have, but they are not aggressively evangelical in nature. The primary philosophy behind wisdom religions is a type of self-worship, wherein the primary goal is to improve oneself to some ultimate end, i.e., achieving godhood or enlightenment.

Because the focus of wisdom religions is introspection and self-elevation through meditation, they tend to attract followers even if they aren't evangelical in the classic sense of the word.

In the second century, a variety of Gnostic cults arose—most claiming to be the true Christianity—that subscribed to a type of "Wisdom Religion." These were zealously opposed by the core Christian Church, and eventually diminished.

In modern times, some belief systems calling themselves Christianity have become increasingly spiritualistic in their teachings, practicing a kind of syncretism with New Age religions.

While these forms of "Christianity" are popular at a cultural level, they cannot be reasonably defended from scripture or from church history.

Cults

For the purpose of this study, a cult would be defined as any type of religion that isolates its adherents into a community that discourages or forbids interaction with people or ideas outside of that community, and zealously ostracizes members of that community who doubt the teachings of the cult, express ideas contrary to the teachings of the cult, or leave the cult.

While aspects of what is here defined as a "cult" can be found in almost every world religion, the uniqueness of a cult is that it dictates rather than discusses ideas. There is a small leadership or singular leader who defines the beliefs for the entire community, and members are asked to memorize rather than interact with those ideas.

A disturbing number of cults have spun off from Christian churches over the years, but their teachings and practices are widely errant when compared to broad Biblical teachings and classic Christianity. Many well-meaning Christian groups *do* isolate themselves from the culture in the hopes of maintaining their purity, but this violates the essential principle that Christians are called to be "the salt of the world," "the light of the world," and to "make disciples of all nations."

The Unique Nature of Christianity

While, at one time or other in one iteration or another, Christianity has been called all of the above, it began as the following of one, charismatic leader who was said to have died and risen again.

Unlike a state religion, Christianity, in its original form, had no political power at all, and would continue to be politically powerless for at least 300 years until it became a state religion under Constantine.

Unlike a theocracy, each person was given the unique privilege of direct access to God versus having to rely on a priest to intercede on their behalf. Each person was also held personally responsible for his or her own relationship with God and his or her own spiritual growth.

The original church differed from a cult in several ways: It actively encouraged interaction with the wider culture, independent thinking on the part of the followers, and the leader was, as mentioned above, not present on earth. While the community of the church was told to encourage and guide one another, each Christian was responsible for his or her own faith and relationship with God. The availability of scriptures in the common language was consistently of primary importance, so that any one person could freely examine the claims of scripture and form his or her own conclusions, rather than relying on some dictatorial and unquestionable teacher.

All of the major world religions *except* for Christianity were picked up and developed almost immediately by some group of powerful people. Christianity remained an underdog religion subject to bias, hatred, and torment for nearly three centuries, and yet it survived and flourished all the same.

This remains true of Christianity to this day: practitioners of Christianity in countries that are hostile toward the faith continue to cling doggedly to their beliefs despite the threats of violence and torment they endure.

What, besides truth, could possibly explain the tenacity of Christianity, unique in the milieu of world religions?

Part V
THE EVIDENCE FROM PROPHECY

Chapter 17
JESUS AS THE
FULFILLMENT OF PROPHECY

In the previous sections, we have explored evidence from the New Testament documents, arguing for an early dating and the eyewitness nature of the reports. We argued that the versions of the documents we have are relatively accurate, and we have examined the most liberal viewpoint on the documents to show that, from any perspective, it is evident that Jesus rose from the dead.

We also examined archeological and historical evidence *outside* the New Testament documents to point the fact that Jesus was factual and that the early Christian Church bore testament to that through their actions and their writings.

There is one final category of evidence to indicate that Jesus was who he claimed to be according to the New Testament: Old Testament prophecy.

The Effectiveness of the Argument

One might rightly ask how Old Testament prophecy is a legitimate argument for the truth of Jesus if an unbelieving world doesn't accept that the Old Testament is particularly true in any significant sense.

The reason this argument succeeds is that, inerrant or not, the Old Testament has remained consistently unchanged since before the writing of the New Testament. There are two evidences we can cite to show this: firstly, the Dead Sea Scrolls and, secondly, the Jewish Tanakh.

The Dead Sea Scrolls include a variety of Old Testament documents dated from before the writing of the New Testament that verify their overall consistency with the current version of the Old Testament. The Jewish Tanakh (the Hebrew version of the Old Testament) has been preserved independently of the Christian Old Testament. The Jews have no reason to make their scriptures align with Christian teachings, and very good reasons to make sure it doesn't, yet the Jewish Tanakh is in accord with the Christian Old Testament as well.

This being the case, it cannot be argued that the Old Testament has been altered to match the details of Christ's life and teachings. One could certainly argue that the details of the New Testament were fudged in order to match prophecies and teachings in the Old Testament, but the gaping differences between Jesus of Nazareth and the expectations the Jewish faith has had regarding the Messiah argue against this idea.

Additionally, as we have shown, the copies of the New Testament documents that we have access to would allow for tracking any modifications that might have been made by the church to manipulate them to match Old Testament prophecy, but this does not seem to be the case. Any similarities between Old Testament prophecy and the Jesus of the New Testament appear to have been there since the beginning.

If it can be shown that Jesus fulfills prophecies made in the Old Testament, this lends *supernatural* weight to the argument for Jesus as the son of God and Messiah. This, combined with the evidence for his resurrection, make a cumulative case that Jesus was not just good, but miraculous.

Is Jesus the Jewish Messiah?

The reason the Jewish people reject Jesus as the Messiah is very simple: he did not rise up and take the throne of David, defeating Israel's enemies and establishing it as a kingdom forevermore, as the Tanakh predicted the Messiah would.

In fact, this very problem is recognized throughout the gospels. On several occasions the people, enthralled with Jesus' teachings and deeds, sought to make him king by force, but he always resisted. (John 6:15)

After being captured, John the Baptist's faith in Jesus began to wane, since Jesus had done nothing in the way of taking a kingly stance. John sent his disciples to ask Jesus if he was, in fact, the promised Messiah, or if they should wait for another. (Luke 7:20)

When Jesus announced to his disciples that he was going up to Jerusalem to die, Peter rebuked him, saying "Far be it from you, Lord! This shall never happen to you." (Matthew 16:22)

After Jesus' death, especially, his followers all but abandoned faith that he was the Messiah. As his downhearted and disillusioned disciples explained as they traveled to Emmaus, "Concerning Jesus of Nazareth, a man who was a prophet mighty in deed and word before God and all the people, and how our chief priests and rulers delivered him up to be condemned to death, and crucified him. But we had hoped that he was the one to redeem Israel." (Luke 24:19)

This concept that the Messiah should rightfully take the throne of David, and Jesus did not do that, is not glossed over in the New Testament at all. In fact, it is one of the major struggles for those Jews who regarded this deeply confusing Jesus who, at the same time, taught and acted like the Messiah, and yet took a passive role, avoiding any political entanglements and humbly proceeding to his own death.

Can such a person be reconciled with the Old Testament Messiah?

On the road to Emmaus, the disguised Jesus responded to his disillusioned disciples this way:

> ""O foolish ones, and slow of heart to believe all that the prophets have spoken! Was it not necessary that the Christ should suffer these things and enter into his glory?" And beginning with Moses and all the Prophets, he interpreted to them in all the Scriptures the things concerning himself." (Luke 24:25-27)

The claim here being that Jesus' life, death, and resurrection *was*, in fact, consistent with Old Testament prophecy.

While it is all very well and good to make a nebulous claim that the Old Testament Messiah is consistent with Jesus, it remains to be shown how this is, and how one would address the primary objection: Why isn't Jesus sitting in the throne of David?

The claim of the New Testament is that, firstly, Jesus' death and resurrection were a necessary precursor to his coming to reign; and secondly that he will, in fact, take the throne of David at some point in the future. This can be seen in such passages as this:

Acts 1:6-7
English Standard Version (ESV)

The Ascension

⁶ So when they had come together, they asked him, "Lord, will you at this time restore the kingdom to Israel?" ⁷ He said to them, "It is not for you to know times or seasons that the Father has fixed by his own authority."

Here the disciples ask, and Jesus implicitly acknowledges, that he will "restore the kingdom to Israel," but that the information on *when* this will happen is not yet revealed.

On this point, Jews and Christians agree: The Messiah is coming to take the throne of David at some point in the future— the disagreement being on the identity of this Messiah. Christians believe the coming Messiah is also Jesus of Nazareth. Jews do not.

If Jesus *did*, indeed, rise from the dead, then it is at least possible that he is also the coming Messiah as Christians believe. The question becomes—disregarding for a moment the possible future return of Jesus as Messiah—was Jesus' life and death consistent with what the Old Testament has to say regarding the coming Messiah?

Setting the precedent

Immediately prior to his crucifixion, Jesus rode into Jerusalem with people laying their coats before him, and shouting "Hosanna to the Son of David! Blessed is he who comes in the name of the Lord! Hosanna in the highest!" (Matthew 21:9) Literally overnight, these same people were shouting "Crucify him!" to the Roman official (Mark 15:13). If Jesus was, indeed, the Messiah, would his own people so quickly turn on him, reject him, and send him to his death?

In the book of Acts, a Jewish Christian named Stephen delivers a speech in which he takes his Jewish audience through a thumbnail sketch of their history, highlighting the struggles and rejection that their leaders and prophets endured. He concludes his sermon this way:

Acts 7:51-53
English Standard Version (ESV)

[51] "You stiff-necked people, uncircumcised in heart and ears, you always resist the Holy Spirit. As your fathers did, so do you. [52] Which of the prophets did

your fathers not persecute? And they killed those who announced beforehand the coming of the Righteous One, whom you have now betrayed and murdered, [53] you who received the law as delivered by angels and did not keep it."

The point Stephen makes here is valid: When examined, practically every great prophet and leader in Jewish history was rejected and opposed *before* they were embraced:

The most celebrated of the prophets, Elijah, lived as a constant fugitive, living in the desert, dressing in animal skins, and eating what little he could find to survive, knowing that if he were to show his face in civilization, the powers that be would have him killed. This same man is now celebrated in Jewish culture as the prophet who will return to herald the coming of the Messiah, and they set an extra place at the table for him every time they celebrate the Passover.

Jeremiah, "The Weeping Prophet," spent his entire ministry pleading with the people of Israel to repent and prophesying the coming Babylonian captivity. He received not a single convert, and tradition tells that his life ended in a brutal death where his own countrymen sawed his body in half. Now his "Lamentations" are read as a yearly meditation over the destruction of Jerusalem.

Moses, the Lawgiver and Emancipator, was mocked and run out of Egypt by his own people on his first foray into their liberation. He spent forty years as a lowly shepherd before God brought him back to free his people.

The Messianic King David was anointed for kinghood by the prophet Samuel while he was just a boy, decades before he actually became the king. David spent most of the interceding years on the run for his life as his own King Saul hunted him down.

Even after assuming the throne, David was forced to flee his kingdom and almost lost his reign in a bloody coup incited by his own son.

But perhaps the most telling example is that of Joseph. As a boy, Joseph received a prophetic vision that he would one day assume a position of power wherein his family would bow before him. These visions were poorly received by the family, and his brothers eventually conspired to beat him, bind him, and sell him into slavery for twenty pieces of silver (a very direct parallel to Jesus' betrayal).

Through a series of unusual circumstances, Joseph eventually ended up in a position of power second only to the most powerful man in the world at that time—years after his brothers sold him as a slave.

When his brothers found themselves kneeling before this man who revealed himself as their brother, they met the revelation with a mixture of fear and sorrow. It is telling, then, that the Old Testament prophet, Zechariah, described Israel's response to the arrival of their Messiah the same way:

Zechariah 12:7-10
English Standard Version (ESV)

7 "And the LORD will give salvation to the tents of Judah first, that the glory of the house of David and the glory of the inhabitants of Jerusalem may not surpass that of Judah. 8 On that day the LORD will protect the inhabitants of Jerusalem, so that the feeblest among them on that day shall be like David, and the house of David shall be like God, like the angel of the LORD, going before them. 9 And on that day I will seek to destroy all the nations that come against Jerusalem.

10 "And I will pour out on the house of David and the inhabitants of Jerusalem a spirit of grace and pleas for mercy, so that, *when they look on me, on him whom they have pierced, they shall mourn for him, as*

one mourns for an only child, and weep bitterly over him, as one weeps over a firstborn.

Viewed on its own, this passage is deeply confusing. At one moment it is talking of a conquering Messiah destroying the enemies of his people, taking the throne of David, and strengthening the people "like David." The next moment it is talking of the people of Israel looking "on him whom they have pierced" and mourning and weeping "as one weeps over a firstborn."

For a Christian, there is no ambiguity whatsoever in this passage, but divorced from Jesus, this passage presents a puzzling mystery that is not easily explained.

The concept of the Messiah having to suffer in order to triumph is, of course, one of the primary themes of the New Testament:

Hebrews 12:2
English Standard Version (ESV)

²looking to Jesus, the founder and perfecter of our faith, who for the joy that was set before him endured the cross, despising the shame, and is seated at the right hand of the throne of God.

A victory without struggle is a hollow victory:

Philippians 2:6-11
English Standard Version (ESV)

⁶who, though he was in the form of God, did not count equality with God a thing to be grasped, ⁷but emptied himself, by taking the form of a servant, being born in the likeness of men. ⁸And being found in human form, he humbled himself by becoming obedient to the point of death, even death on a cross. ⁹*Therefore*

God has highly exalted him and bestowed on him the name that is above every name, ¹⁰so that at the name of Jesus every knee should bow, in heaven and on earth and under the earth, ¹¹and every tongue confess that Jesus Christ is Lord, to the glory of God the Father.

However, it is not merely the New Testament that presents the concept that the Messiah must suffer before he receives glory. Isaiah 53 reveals that the Messiah would be rejected:

Isaiah 53:3

³ He was despised and rejected by men; a man of sorrows, and acquainted with grief; and as one from whom men hide their faces he was despised, and we esteemed him not.

...would suffer:

Isaiah 53:5

⁵ But he was pierced for our transgressions; he was crushed for our iniquities; upon him was the chastisement that brought us peace, and with his wounds we are healed.

...would die:

Isaiah 53:9

⁹ And they made his grave with the wicked and with a rich man in his death, although he had done no violence, and there was no deceit in his mouth.

And through suffering and death, would triumph:

Isaiah 53:10-12

[10] Yet it was the will of the LORD to crush him; he has put him to grief; when his soul makes an offering for guilt, he shall see his offspring; he shall prolong his days; the will of the LORD shall prosper in his hand. [11] Out of the anguish of his soul he shall see and be satisfied; by his knowledge shall the righteous one, my servant, make many to be accounted righteous, and he shall bear their iniquities. [12] *Therefore I will divide him a portion with the many, and he shall divide the spoil with the strong,* because he poured out his soul to death and was numbered with the transgressors; yet he bore the sin of many, and makes intercession for the transgressors.

Old Testament Prophecies that indicate Jesus

While Jewish scholars would fail to agree, there are a number of Messianic prophecies from the Old Testament that are suspiciously similar to the person of Jesus of Nazareth.

1. Born in Bethlehem

In the second chapter of the book of *Matthew*, it records that some wise men arrived at the palace of King Herod requesting to know where the King of the Jews had been born.

King Herod was historically a very paranoid and, frankly, insane man. Historically, he is well known for his violent measures to protect his throne, including the banishing of his first wife and his infant son, executing his second wife and several members of his family, and arresting anyone who publicly spoke out against him (Cohen, Shaye. "Roman Domination: The Jewish Revolt and the

Destruction of the Second Temple," in *Ancient Israel*, ed. Hershel Shanks. (Biblical Archaeology Society, 1999), p. 271.).

A true example of Herod's irrational, murderous insanity is recorded by Josephus in his *Antiquities*. He writes that as Herod was on his deathbed, he ordered a large group of distinguished Jewish leaders to come to Jericho where he was dying. He instructed his soldiers to slaughter the leaders as soon as he died to ensure that there would be mourning in Judea when he died. Fortunately for the Jews, they did not comply with this order.

Taking this into account, it is not out of character for Herod to conspire to kill this prophesied "King of the Jews" upon his birth. Matthew tells that the Jewish scholars under Herod's command searched the scriptures and determined that the Messiah would be born in Bethlehem. The Old Testament passage to which they referred was Micah 5:2 which reads:

Micah 5:2
English Standard Version (ESV)

[2] But you, O Bethlehem Ephrathah, who are too little to be among the clans of Judah, from you shall come forth for me one who is to be ruler in Israel, <u>whose coming forth is from of old, from ancient days</u>.

It is difficult to interpret this verse as referring to anyone *but* the Messiah, considering the description given of him. Since both Luke and Matthew record that Jesus was born in Bethlehem, this would either be a fairly extraordinary coincidence (in the first century, the population of Bethlehem was very small) or it indicates Jesus as Messiah.

2. The Virgin Birth

Both Matthew and Luke report that Jesus was born of a virgin. It is difficult to say whether or not Rabbis would have looked for this in the Messiah, but in retrospect, it definitely fits several prophecies made in the Old Testament.

The first of these is in Genesis 3:15. In this passage, God is doling out penalties for the rebellion of Adam and Eve, and the deception of the serpent. Many Christian theologians believe that God's curse toward the serpent is a prophecy of the coming of the Messiah and of his redemptive work:

Genesis 3:15
English Standard Version (ESV)

[15] I will put enmity between you and the woman, and between your offspring and her offspring; he shall bruise your head, and you shall bruise his heel."

The reference to the offspring bruising the serpent's head is taken to indicate Jesus crushing Satan, and the reference to the serpent bruising the heel is taken to indicate the sacrifice Jesus needed to make on the cross. However the really interesting feature of this passage is the word "offspring." In the original Hebrew, this word is literally "seed." When this word is used figuratively for offspring, it is always used in reference to the *male* contribution to reproduction, not the female. This Hebrew word for offspring only references a woman once in scripture, and it is this passage. That a woman would have "seed" without intercourse could very well indicate a virgin birth.

However, perhaps this is too thin a premise upon which to base this prophecy. A much stronger case can be made from Isaiah 7:14, which reads:

Isaiah 7:14
English Standard Version (ESV)

[14] Therefore the Lord himself will give you a sign. Behold, the virgin shall conceive and bear a son, and shall call his name Immanuel.

This is the verse that Matthew cites in his gospel to support the prophetic fulfillment of the virgin birth. In the context of *Isaiah*, God was promising the king that he would destroy the nation that was threatening Israel. To verify this, God told the king to ask for a sign. The king refused, and God expressed displeasure at his refusal. God then told the king that the sign would be a virgin conceiving.

There are a few objections to this passage referring to Jesus. The first is that this sign was promised hundreds of years before Jesus was actually born. The king, the prophet, and everyone who would have benefitted from this sign would be long dead. Therefore, it could not possibly be referring to Jesus. Or could it?

In the broader context of the passage, it is important to note that God was displeased with the king for not asking a sign. It says:

Isaiah 7:10-13
English Standard Version (ESV)

The Sign of Immanuel

[10] Again the LORD spoke to Ahaz, [11] "Ask a sign of the LORD your God; let it be deep as Sheol or high as heaven." [12] But Ahaz said, "I will not ask, and I will not put the LORD to the test." [13] And he said, "Hear then, O house of David! Is it too little for you to weary men, that you weary my God also?"

The sign that God offers, he tells that it will be fulfilled at a far-future time. He says:

Isaiah 7:16
English Standard Version (ESV)

[16] For before the boy knows how to refuse the evil and choose the good, the land whose two kings you dread will be deserted.

The sign God offers won't be fulfilled until the land of the enemy is entirely deserted. The birth of Jesus, several hundred years later, is consistent with this sign, *and* with the fact that Ahaz refused to request the sign for himself.

The second objection to this prophecy is that the Hebrew word for "virgin" could also be translated "young woman." The problem with this objection is that, for a young woman to conceive and bear a child is no miraculous sign at all. It would be impossible to tell if the "sign" had come true or not with young women conceiving every day. The other problem with this objection is that the boy born was to be called "Immanuel," that is, "God with us," is taken by Christians to be a fairly clear reference to the incarnation.

In the late second century BCE, a group of seventy Hebrew scholars collaborated to create an authorized and accurate interpretation of the Hebrew Tanakh in the Greek language. This translation is known as the Septuagint (Latin for "Seventy") or abbreviated LXX. The Hebrew word in the Isaiah 7 passage—which could be "virgin" or "young, unmarried woman"—is *almah*. The LXX translates *almah* as *parthenos*, which is Greek for a literal "virgin." Since this translation was made well before Jesus was born, it is evident that early Hebrews took this prophecy to mean a literal virgin.

Possibly most significantly, however, is the fact that Matthew took this to be a fulfillment of prophecy. There is very little question that the book of *Matthew* was written by a Jew based on the reasons discussed in Chapter 7. It is unlikely that he would have made this connection between Jesus' virgin birth and the Isaiah prophecy if the Jews did not take the world "virgin" literally.

3. Line of Messianic descent

There is no question whatsoever about the line of Messianic descent. Throughout scripture, the theme of God narrowing the line of descent by selecting particular people and rejecting others to deliver the Messiah is consistent. In Genesis, the descendants of Adam's son, Seth, were claimed to be righteous before God (Genesis 4:26). One of these descendants was Noah, who, along with his sons, were the last people left alive on earth after the flood. Of Noah's three sons, Shem was given the blessing over his brothers (Genesis 9:26).

One of Shem's descendants was Abraham, who was called rather suddenly by God to separate himself and walk before God (Genesis 12:1). Abraham is promised by God that all the families of the earth will be blessed through him (Genesis 12:3, 22:18). Abraham had two sons, and Isaac is selected to carry this blessing (Genesis 17:19, 21:12). Isaac had two sons, and Jacob was chosen over his elder brother to carry the birthright (Genesis 25:33) and the blessing (Genesis 27).

In the book of Numbers, the gentile prophet of the Lord who, against his will, was forced to bless Israel by God when he was attempting to curse them, made a very clear messianic blessing toward Jacob:

Numbers 24:17
English Standard Version (ESV)

¹⁷ I see him, but not now; I behold him, but not near:
a star shall come out of Jacob, and a scepter shall
rise out of Israel; it shall crush the forehead of Moab
and break down all the sons of Sheth.

Jacob (renamed "Israel" by God) had twelve sons (each of whom fathered one of the twelve tribes). Of his twelve sons, Judah was selected to carry the scepter (Genesis 49:10).

However, the nation of Israel did not actually have a king for several hundred years *after* Judah was offered the scepter. True to form, two men were anointed for kinghood, the first, Saul, was rejected by the Lord, and the second, David, from the tribe of Judah, received God's covenant to become the line through which the Messiah would be conceived (2 Samuel 7:12-13) and the throne Messiah would take (Isaiah 9:7).

Both Matthew and Luke take pains to trace Jesus' lineage as far back as Adam. This was clearly in order to show that he descended through the exact order of descent that God provided for the Messiah.

4. Messiah would be rejected by his own people.

Any conception of the Messiah that does not also include him being rejected at some point does not take the full scope of scripture into account. The clearest passage regarding this rejection is, of course, Isaiah 53. This passage details the Messiah's rejection *and* the abuse that he received. It clearly states:

Isaiah 53:2-3
English Standard Version (ESV)

[2] For he grew up before him like a young plant, and like a root out of dry ground; he had no form or majesty that we should look at him, and no beauty that we should desire him.

[3] He was despised and rejected by men; a man of sorrows, and acquainted with grief; and as one from whom men hide their faces he was despised, *and we esteemed him not.*

By using the first person plural, this prophecy indicates that he is rejected by the Jews specifically.

Another prophecy of the Messiah's rejection is the sixty-ninth Psalm, where the Psalmist says:

Psalm 69:8
English Standard Version (ESV)

[8] I have become a stranger to my brothers, an alien to my mother's sons.

5. The Psalms

Both Hebrew and Christian scholars believe that the Davidic Psalms have strongly Messianic themes. In the book of Matthew, Jesus makes this argument from one of the Davidic Psalms:

Matthew 22:41-46
New International Version (NIV)

Whose Son Is the Messiah?

[41] While the Pharisees were gathered together, Jesus asked them, [42] "What do you think about the Messiah? Whose son is he?"

"The son of David," they replied.

[43] He said to them, "How is it then that David, speaking by the Spirit, calls him 'Lord'? For he says,

[44] "'The Lord said to my Lord: "Sit at my right hand until I put your enemies under your feet."'

[45] If then David calls him 'Lord,' how can he be his son?" [46] No one could say a word in reply, and from that day on no one dared to ask him any more questions.

Jesus is suggesting that David was prophetically speaking of the Messiah in this Psalm, and the Pharisees agreed. The Psalm he was quoting is this:

Psalm 110
New International Version (NIV)

Psalm 110

Of David. A psalm.

[1] The LORD says to my lord:

"Sit at my right hand until I make your enemies a footstool for your feet."

[2] The LORD will extend your mighty scepter from Zion, saying, "Rule in the midst of your enemies!"

[3] Your troops will be willing on your day of battle. Arrayed in holy splendor, your young men will come to you like dew from the morning's womb.

[4] The LORD has sworn and will not change his mind: "You are a priest forever, in the order of Melchizedek."

[5] The Lord is at your right hand; he will crush kings on the day of his wrath.

[6] He will judge the nations, heaping up the dead and crushing the rulers of the whole earth.

[7] He will drink from a brook along the way, and so he will lift his head high.

There can be very little doubt that this Psalm references the coming of the Messiah and the day of his triumph.

Considering how much the Davidic Psalms speak to the Messiah, it is interesting, therefore, to see how much of what is contained in the Davidic Psalms closely resembles events in Jesus life:

1. *The driving out of the money changers:* In the well-known story of Jesus attacking and driving the money changers out of the temple, Matthew says references Psalm 69:9 which says "for zeal from your house consumes me"

2. *Vinegar on the cross:* As Jesus hung on the cross, he said "I thirst." Psalm 69:3 says "I am worn out calling for help; my throat is parched." When Jesus mentioned his thirst, those at the cross raised a sponge soaked in vinegar for him to drink. Psalm 69:21 says "They ... gave me vinegar for my thirst"

3. *Psalm 22:* In the original Hebrew, Psalms were not numbered. Rather, the first line of the Psalm was considered the title of that Psalm. On the cross, Christ is quoted as crying "My God, My God, why have you forsaken me?" This utterance is the first line—the title—of the twenty-second Psalm.

It is significant, then, than the twenty-second Psalm contains a number of references to what happened to Jesus on the cross.

Psalm 22:7-8 read:

"All who see me mock me; they make mouths at me; they wag their heads; [8] "He trusts in the LORD; let him deliver him; let him rescue him, for he delights in him!""

197

Matthew 27:39-40 states:

[39] And those who passed by derided him, wagging their heads [40] and saying, "You who would destroy the temple and rebuild it in three days, save yourself! If you are the Son of God, come down from the cross."

Psalm 22:16 reads:

"For dogs encompass me; a company of evildoers encircles me; *they have pierced my hands and feet—*"

This could easily be taken as a reference to crucifixion.

Psalm 22:18 reads:

"[18] they divide my garments among them, and for my clothing they cast lots."

Matthew 27:35 states:

"[35] And when they had crucified him, they divided his garments among them by casting lots."

4.   *The betrayal and resurrection of Christ*

Psalm 41:5-13 speak very suggestively about the betrayal and resurrection of Christ:

Psalm 41:5-13
English Standard Version Anglicised (ESVUK)

[5] My enemies say of me in malice, "When will he die,
        and his name perish?"

⁶ And when one comes to see me, he utters empty words, while his heart gathers iniquity; when he goes out, he tells it abroad.

⁷ All who hate me whisper together about me; they imagine the worst for me.

⁸ They say, "A deadly thing is poured out on him; he will not rise again from where he lies."

⁹ Even my close friend in whom I trusted, who ate my bread, has lifted his heel against me.

¹⁰ But you, O Lord, be gracious to me, and raise me up, that I may repay them!

¹¹ By this I know that you delight in me: my enemy will not shout in triumph over me.

¹² But you have upheld me because of my integrity, and set me in your presence for ever.

¹³ Blessed be the Lord, the God of Israel, from everlasting to everlasting! Amen and Amen.

Verse 5 appears to reference the plot against Jesus, along with the frustration that his teachings did not perish with him on the cross.

Verse 6 appears to reference Judas, but Judas is more directly referenced in verse 9 as the "close friend" who "ate my bread" and then betrays.

The enemies say that he "will not rise again from where he lies." The author then asks that God "raise me up" and states that God "set me in your presence for ever." All of which follow suit with what the New Testament said of Jesus' resurrection and ascension.

6. Thirty pieces of Silver and the Potter's Field

There are several Old Testament prophets whom God commanded to perform unusual acts as picture metaphors. Hosea, for instance, was commanded to marry a prostitute in order to display God's feelings about how Israel constantly left him for other gods.

The prophet Zechariah was one such man. Here is one of the things God commanded him to do:

Zechariah 11:12-13
English Standard Version Anglicised (ESVUK)

[12] Then I said to them, "If it seems good to you, give me my wages; but if not, keep them." And they weighed out as my wages thirty pieces of silver. [13] Then the LORD said to me, "Throw it to the potter"—the lordly price at which I was priced by them. So I took the thirty pieces of silver and threw them into the house of the LORD, to the potter.

Here the merchant willingly sets the price of thirty pieces of silver, which God calls "the lordly price at which I was priced by them." Then he tells Zechariah to "Throw it to the potter."

Of course, in the betrayal of Christ, Judas sold him for thirty pieces of silver (the lordly price at which I was priced by them), which, when he threw it back at the feet of the Sanhedrin, was then used to purchase a potter's field.

7. Abuse at the hands of his people

After he was arrested, the Gospels describe that Christ was mocked (Matthew 26:68), spat upon (Matthew 26:67), whipped, and had his beard pulled out.

This description is preempted in the prophecy of Isaiah, in his "servant song," which has been interpreted as coming from the perspective of the Messiah:

Isaiah 50:6
English Standard Version (ESV)

[6] I gave my back to those who strike, and my cheeks to those who pull out the beard; I hid not my face from disgrace and spitting.

8. Isaiah 53

The clearest, most unambiguous prophecy of Jesus is Isaiah chapter 53, which succinctly summarizes Jesus' persecution and death for sins. So much of Jesus' life is contained in this chapter:

1. *He was rejected by his own people*

The Prophecy:

Isaiah 53:3
English Standard Version (ESV)

[3] He was despised and rejected by men; a man of sorrows, and acquainted with grief; and as one from whom men hide their faces he was despised, and we esteemed him not.

The fulfillment:

John 1:11
English Standard Version (ESV)

[11] He came to his own, and his own people did not receive him.

2.   *He was pierced and wounded*

The Prophecy

Isaiah 53:5
English Standard Version (ESV)

⁵ But he was pierced for our transgressions; he was crushed for our iniquities; upon him was the chastisement that brought us peace, and with his wounds we are healed.

The Fulfillment

John 19:34
English Standard Version (ESV)

³⁴ But one of the soldiers pierced his side with a spear, and at once there came out blood and water.

3.   *He was silent before his accusers*

The Prophecy

Isaiah 53:7
English Standard Version (ESV)

⁷ He was oppressed, and he was afflicted, yet he opened not his mouth; like a lamb that is led to the slaughter, and like a sheep that before its shearers is silent, so he opened not his mouth.

The Fulfillment

Luke 23:9-10
English Standard Version (ESV)

⁹ So he questioned him at some length, but he made no answer. ¹⁰ The chief priests and the scribes stood by, vehemently accusing him.

4. *He was judged and taken away*

The Prophecy

Isaiah 53:8
English Standard Version (ESV)

⁸ By oppression and judgment he was taken away; and as for his generation, who considered that he was cut off out of the land of the living, stricken for the transgression of my people?

The Fulfillment

Luke 22:52-54
English Standard Version (ESV)

⁵² Then Jesus said to the chief priests and officers of the temple and elders, who had come out against him, "Have you come out as against a robber, with swords and clubs? ⁵³ When I was with you day after day in the temple, you did not lay hands on me. But this is your hour, and the power of darkness."

⁵⁴ Then they seized him and led him away, bringing him into the high priest's house, and Peter was following at a distance.

5. *He was buried in a rich man's tomb*

The Prophecy

Isaiah 53:9
English Standard Version (ESV)

[9] And they made his grave with the wicked and with a rich man in his death, although he had done no violence, and there was no deceit in his mouth.

The Fulfillment

Matthew 27:57-60
English Standard Version (ESV)

Jesus Is Buried

[57] When it was evening, there came a rich man from Arimathea, named Joseph, who also was a disciple of Jesus. [58] He went to Pilate and asked for the body of Jesus. Then Pilate ordered it to be given to him. [59] And Joseph took the body and wrapped it in a clean linen shroud [60] and laid it in his own new tomb, which he had cut in the rock. And he rolled a great stone to the entrance of the tomb and went away.

Jesus himself even referenced the prophecy of Isaiah 53 as referring to him. In Luke 22:37, he references Isaiah 53:12 when he says:

Luke 22:37
English Standard Version (ESV)

For I tell you that this Scripture must be fulfilled in me: 'And he was numbered with the transgressors.' For what is written about me has its fulfillment."

Even if it were shown that many of these prophecies related to something other than Jesus, only one of them has to reference Jesus in order to show that he is the Messiah, or at the very least, miraculous. One would have to prove that every single one of these prophecies has to do with something besides Jesus of Nazareth.

Conclusion

The Jewish idea of the Messiah as the conquering king who takes the throne of David is not fundamentally in conflict with the Christian view that Jesus will return to take the throne of David. The idea of the struggle, rejection, and then triumph of the Messiah is also consistent with the pattern and prophecy of the Old Testament. More than this, however, Jesus of Nazareth, his life, death and resurrection, make sense of a number of otherwise mysterious prophecies about the Messiah.

Jews do not universally reject the idea of Jesus as Messiah. Christianity is, at its root, a Jewish religion that has welcomed Gentiles into it; and some of the most profound Christian theologians have been and continue to be Jews.

Immediately prior to his crucifixion, Jesus looked down on the city of Jerusalem and uttered this lament:

Matthew 23:37-39
English Standard Version (ESV)

Lament over Jerusalem

[37] "O Jerusalem, Jerusalem, the city that kills the prophets and stones those who are sent to it! How often would I have gathered your children together as a hen gathers her brood under her wings, and you were not willing! [38] See, your house is left to you desolate. [39] For I tell you, you will not see me again, until you say, 'Blessed is he who comes in the name of the Lord.'"

Jesus tells here that he *will* one day be accepted and welcomed by the Jewish people. Just like Moses, David, and Joseph, the people who once denied him will welcome him as their ruler and liberator.

The Christian message, in brief, is that Jesus—as a perfect, sinless individual—substituted himself for imperfect and wicked humankind, taking on the penalty of sin so that imperfect humans could escape God's righteous judgment by appealing to his sacrifice. Is this understanding, however, consistent with the Old Testament concept of the Jewish Messiah? If it is not, then the Old Testament texts have no place in the Christian canon and Jews are justified in rejecting Jesus as their Messiah.

We examine this question next.

Chapter 18
JESUS AS SUBSTITUTIONARY SACRIFICE

Acceptable Sacrifice

As the book of Genesis traces the origin of the Jewish people, the very first animal sacrifice to be mentioned was that of Abel in the infamous "Cain and Abel" narrative. In this narrative, Cain's sacrifice of the fruits of his harvest was denied by God, while Abel's sacrifice of the "firstborn of his flock" was accepted. While much ink has been spilled in trying to explain why one sacrifice was acceptable and one was not, the salient point here is that such sacrifices *had to be acceptable* to God. One could not offer simply anything in any way and expect this offering to work.

Another point from this narrative worth noting is that Abel's acceptable sacrifice was "the firstborn." This theme of a firstborn sacrifice is repeated again and again throughout the Old Testament.

Substitutionary Sacrifice

The fifteenth chapter of Genesis tells the story of God (Yahweh) coming to Abram (Abraham) and promising him the inheritance of the land of Canaan. This is, by this time, no new message to Abram. God has promised this several times before. Abram despairs, however, in believing because he and his wife are now very elderly and have never had any children to which they can pass an inheritance.

In order to reassure Abram that he will fulfill his promise, God enacts what, to modern eyes, looks like a bizarre ritual. He commands that Abram bring a number of domestic animals, cut them each in half, and create a corridor between the animal halves through which he can walk.

Of this ritual, Bible scholar John MacArthur writes:

> The sign of ancient covenants often involved the cutting in half of animals, so that the pledging parties could walk between them, affirming that the same should happen to them if they broke the covenant. (MacAuthur, The MacAuthur Bible Commentary, 2005, page 35)

This is a window into the ancient idea of animal sacrifice: the animals are substitutes for the people they represent.

The book of Job is frequently considered the most ancient text contained in the Hebrew Tanakh. In the very first chapter of this ancient text, the titular character is seen offering burnt sacrifices to God to consecrate his children because "It may be that my children have sinned, and cursed God in their hearts." (Job 1:5)

This idea of animals taking the place of humans for God's judgment is clearly as ancient as the most ancient of historical documents.

A significant portion of the book of Genesis is devoted to the person of Abraham, and with good cause. Abraham is considered to be the father of the Jewish people and is called the "Friend of God" (James 2:23). One of the stories from Abraham's life that is well known to almost everyone is the sacrifice of his son Isaac (Genesis 22).

God had promised to give Abraham a son by his wife, Sarah. However, this son was a long time coming, and decades elapsed before God finally fulfilled this promise. What is more, God specifically told Abraham that an entire nation of people would be born through Isaac, the promised son, and his first and only son through his legitimate wife, Sarah (Abraham's actual first son was illegitimate and denied the promise).

It is quite a surprise, therefore, when God tells Abraham to take Isaac up onto a hill and sacrifice him. This command appears to run contrary to everything God has promised Abraham before. Abraham is obedient, however. He takes his son to the hill and when his son asks where the sacrifice is, Abraham responds by saying "God will provide for himself the lamb" (Genesis 22:8). Just as he is about to plunge the knife into Isaac, God tells him to stop, and indicates a nearby goat that happens to be trapped in a thorn bush by its horns as a substitute for sacrificing Isaac.

There are a great many interesting points to this story. It has the theme of a firstborn son who is the promised heir being sacrificed, and it has the theme of a substitute sacrifice, provided by God, taking the place of the individual, and thereby sparing him from his fate.

The concept of animal sacrifice as it is practiced in the Jewish faith is really first explored in the Passover narrative (Exodus 12). In this passage, God has already sent 9 plagues upon Egypt in the effort to convince the pharaoh to release the captive Jews. As the pharaoh has continued to refuse, God threatens the final plague, which differs significantly from the first nine:

Exodus 11:4-7
English Standard Version (ESV)

"So Moses said, 'Thus says the LORD: About midnight I will go out in the midst of Egypt, and every firstborn in the land of Egypt shall die, from the firstborn of Pharaoh who sits on the throne, even to the firstborn of the slave girl who is behind the handmill, and all the firstborn of the cattle. There shall be a great cry throughout all the land of Egypt, such as there has never been, nor ever will be again. But not a dog shall growl against any of the people of Israel, either man or beast, that you may know that the LORD makes a distinction between Egypt and Israel.'"

In the previous plagues, the "distinction between Egypt and Israel" was made automatically: the plague would specifically avoid the region wherein the Israelites stayed. In this plague, however, God prescribed a ritual that the Israelites were commanded to follow so as not to become victims of the plague:

Exodus 12:21-23
English Standard Version (ESV)

"Then Moses called all the elders of Israel and said to them, 'Go and select lambs for yourselves according to your clans, and kill the Passover lamb. Take a bunch of hyssop and dip it in the blood that is in the basin, and touch the lintel and the two doorposts with the blood that is in the basin. None of you shall go out of the door of his house until the morning. For the LORD will pass through to strike the Egyptians, and when he sees the blood on the lintel and on the two doorposts, the LORD will pass over the door and will not allow the destroyer to enter your houses to strike you.'"

This Passover feast is established as the most significant ongoing ritual that the Jews observe to this day.

Here it is established that the sacrifice must be a male lamb without blemish, and that the blood specifically will be the sign, causing the wrath of God to pass over. What is significant about this plague is that, once again, it is the firstborn that is in danger of death. This and the Passover ritual itself create a very remarkable parallel to the idea that a perfect sacrifice of a firstborn son will save imperfect people from God's wrath. Moreover, it is significant that Jesus was crucified during Passover when the lambs were being slaughtered.

Later, the Mosaic law elaborates on the concept of blood sacrifices being performed routinely in order to obtain God's forgiveness for sin, the descriptions of how to carry out these rituals taking up a significant portion of the Levitical books.

The Priesthood of the Messiah

The brief 110th Psalm is very Messianic in nature:

Psalm 110
English Standard Version (ESV)

Sit at My Right Hand

A Psalm of David

110 The LORD says to my Lord: "Sit at my right hand, until I make your enemies your footstool."

[2] The LORD sends forth from Zion your mighty scepter. Rule in the midst of your enemies!

[3] Your people will offer themselves freely on the day of your power, in holy garments; from the womb of the morning, the dew of your youth will be yours.

[4] The LORD has sworn and will not change his mind, "You are a priest forever after the order of Melchizedek."

⁵ The Lord is at your right hand; he will shatter kings
on the day of his wrath.

⁶ He will execute judgment among the nations, filling
them with corpses; he will shatter chiefs over
the wide earth.

⁷ He will drink from the brook by the way; therefore
he will lift up his head.

The New Testament makes numerous references to this
Psalm. Jesus uses the first verse as an argument for the Messiah
being the literal "Son of God" (Luke 20:41-44), and the book of
Hebrews spends a great deal of time elaborating on this text.

The Jewish concept of the Messiah is as a king, and this
Psalm bears that interpretation. David (a Messianic king himself)
calls the Messiah "my Lord," and refers to the Messiah's "scepter"
in addition to the numerous references to the reigning and
conquering of the Messiah.

What makes this particular Messianic text so unusual is
verse 4, wherein the Messiah is called "a priest forever after the
order of Melchizedek." This is the verse upon which the New
Testament book of *Hebrews* camps.

Within the Mosaic system, the duties of kings and priests
represented opposite ends of the spectrum. Kings were required
by their station to enforce the Law and penalties of the Law. Priests,
on the other hand, were required to intercede with God on behalf
of the people for the forgiveness of the people's sins, and it was the
priest alone who was authorized by God to offer sacrifices.

In the Old Testament, King Saul attempts to take on the
priestly duty of animal sacrifice prior to an important battle, and
is harshly punished by God by deposing him as king (1 Samuel 13).
Later down the kingly line, King Uzziah attempted to burn incense
in the temple before God and was punished by being instantly

struck with leprosy, leading to his death (2 Chronicles 26). Kingly duties and priestly duties were intended to be separate, and God would never allow the two to mix. With one exception: the Old Testament character of Melchizedek.

In Genesis 14, the character of Melchizedek is briefly introduced as:

Genesis 14:18
English Standard Version (ESV)

18 And Melchizedek king of Salem brought out bread and wine. (He was priest of God Most High.)

Melchizedek was a contemporary of Abraham, meaning that he was a preJewish (or Gentile) priest and king.

In Jewish terms, kings were to be from the line of Judah, whilst priests were required to be from the tribe of Levi. Melchizedek was an exception to this in that he was specially appointed by God as a priest. Moreover, because of his place in time (preJewish), Melchizedek was a priest of Yahweh who offered sacrifices for all people, not simply Jews.

The priest was the only person who was authorized to offer sacrifices to God. By calling the Messiah a priest as well as a king, David is setting the precedent for an utterly unique Messiah who could be the redemption of sin (through sacrifice) as well as the eternal king of Israel.

Messiah as Sacrifice

As with all good Old Testament arguments for Jesus as Messiah, this one ends with Isaiah 53. This controversial passage insists on a Messiah who suffers and dies for sins.

In this single passage is seen all of the elements viewed in this argument. The suffering servant of this passage is shown to be a substitutionary sacrifice: "All we like sheep have gone astray; we have turned—every one—to his own way; and the LORD has laid on him the iniquity of us all." (vs. 6); and he is shown to be an acceptable sacrifice "Yet it was the will of the LORD to crush him he has put him to grief; when his soul makes an offering for guilt, he shall see his offspring; he shall prolong his days; the will of the LORD shall prosper in his hand."

Conclusion

The Old Testament sets up a scenario wherein constant blood sacrifices have to be offered in order to keep the people in favor with God. If the story skips to the righteous and judgmental Messiah coming in conquest, to reign over Israel, something crucial is lost. All the world that is *not* Israel is lost, breaking one of God's *other* promises to Abraham:

Genesis 12:3
English Standard Version (ESV)

"I will bless those who bless you, and him who dishonors you I will curse, and in you *all the families of the earth shall be blessed.*"

More than this, the people of Israel are stuck in a circumstance wherein they remain unredeemed, subject to constant relapses into disobedience and judgment by a righteous Messiah who cannot countenance evil.

The Christian version robs nothing from the Jewish Messiah. He still comes in glory and righteous judgment to take the throne of David. The Christian view merely adds a crucial feature: Israel, and through it, all the world, is redeemed and may live in perfect unity with a Messiah who is not only judge, but also redeemer. Of that day, the prophet Jeremiah predicts:

Jeremiah 23:6
English Standard Version (ESV)

"In his days Judah will be saved, and Israel will dwell securely. And this is the name by which he will be called: 'The LORD is our righteousness.'"

This passage tells that, with the coming of the Messiah, all of Israel will be seen as righteous before God, not because of any inherent goodness, but because God's righteousness is credited to them: "The LORD is our righteousness." This is the Christian gospel in a nutshell.

The consistent message of divine salvation seen in both Old and New Testaments is, itself, evidence for the truth of Christianity. That a scattering of ancient documents, written across a thousand-year span, should remain so unified in message, should consistently require a perfect, substitutionary sacrifice, should predict and then deliver a Messiah who rights the wrongs of a flawed humanity through his self-sacrifice—this is at least worth some consideration to anyone who doubts the Christian message.

Part VI
SHARING THE GOSPEL APOLOGETICALLY

Chapter 19
STRATEGIES FOR DEFENDING YOUR FAITH

M odern culture is saturated with information (and misinformation) regarding Christian views. It is almost a certainty that any given adult you engage on the subject of religion in general and Christianity in particular has already formed strong opinions on that subject, and is not easily convinced to change his or her mind.

Throughout the book, we have explored a comprehensive case for why Jesus was who he said he was and did what the Bible said he did. Learning these facts, however, and communicating these same facts to a highly opinionated and cynical world are two different challenges. In this section, we will explore techniques for discussing your faith with the world around you.

Looking through your Neighbor's Eyes

Imagine for a moment that you are sitting at a meal and are suddenly interrupted by a knock at your door. When you open it, there stand two well-dressed young men with pamphlets in hand. If you are like most people, there is an immediate feeling of annoyance. You know you are about to be preached at about something you have already dismissed as being untrue and unsettling. Your impulse will be to get out of the conversation as quickly as possible.

This is the same experience non-Christians often have when a Christian begins an evangelical conversation with them. They are not interested in what the Christian has to say, they are already certain they don't believe it, and they simply want to end the conversation.

What all people everywhere *are* interested in, however, is sharing their own opinion on things. When you engage a non-Christian on the topic of religion, you have the goal in mind of communicating your worldview and getting them to rationally consider it. They have the same goal in mind. If you wish for them to pay you respect and to consider what you have to say, it is only fair that you pay them the same respect. In this section, we will look at effective ways of doing so.

1 Peter 3

In the first section of this book, we mentioned that 1 Peter 3:15 is a sort of rallying cry for Apologists. However the entire third chapter of 1 Peter (starting at verse 8) is worth a look when it comes to Apologetic tactics. Here's what it tells us.

How Christians act

1 Peter 3:8
English Standard Version (ESV)

[8] Finally, all of you, have unity of mind, sympathy, brotherly love, a tender heart, and a humble mind.

One of the main things that deter people from Christianity is Christian behavior. Accusations of hypocrisy, division, and self-righteous arrogance are a common complaint against Christians. Frequently, these accusations are accurate and justified. In his epistles, John continually stresses that Christians need to be loving toward one another, and that such love is the evidence of their faith and belief. No matter how logical a person may be, they are never going to embrace a system of belief that appears to produce irascible character in people.

Christianity is the belief that you, the individual, are guilty of crimes against the Creator of the universe. Christians acknowledge their sin, repent, and submit themselves to the mercy of God. This is, in fact, a very humbling belief. Those who claim to be Christians and use this to justify some kind of self-righteous arrogance are acting in opposition to the actual teachings of Christianity.

If a person wants to produce a convincing case for Christianity, he or she is *required* to act in love and humility, especially towards other Christians.

It should be added, however, that this should not be done legalistically. Christians are under grace. They fail, sin, and make mistakes like everyone else. The key difference is that Christians are aware of their failings, leading to humility; and of the forgiveness they receive in God, leading to gratitude.

Be Kind when Discussing your Faith

1 Peter 3:9-14
English Standard Version (ESV)

[9] Do not repay evil for evil or reviling for reviling, but on the contrary, bless, for to this you were called, that you may obtain a blessing. [10] For

"Whoever desires to love life and see good days, let him keep his tongue from evil and his lips from speaking deceit; [11] let him turn away from evil and do good; let him seek peace and pursue it. [12] For the eyes of the Lord are on the righteous, and his ears are open to their prayer. But the face of the Lord is against those who do evil."

[13] Now who is there to harm you if you are zealous for what is good? [14] But even if you should suffer for righteousness' sake, you will be blessed. Have no fear of them, nor be troubled,

Discussions of faith and worldviews are prone to being heated. Often, people can become very accusatory and aggressive when their firmly held ideas and convictions are being challenged; or when confronting an idea against which they have strong feelings. This includes both the Christian and the non-Christian in the discussion. How you act towards the other person in the discussion is as important as what you say. If the Christian ends up in a shouting match—using sarcasm, cheap shots, and putdowns toward the other person—he or she does nothing to show the virtue of his or her worldview. It is difficult to bear up under verbal abuse without lashing back, but acting this way will make the other person *more* opposed to your worldview, and it is proof to them that your worldview has no power to improve your behavior.

Instead, it would be wise to heed Peter's warning here and "do not repay evil for evil or reviling for reviling."

Disarming the situation

When the other person starts to become aggressive, it is often helpful to apologize if they feel you were being offensive, and remind them you are not attacking them. This does two things: it establishes your stance as a friendly one, and it reminds them that they are getting aggressive themselves without actually accusing them of anything.

Do not do an information dump

During the course of this study, we have reviewed a robust case for Jesus and his resurrection. This information is very important in addressing the doubts and misgivings of nonbelievers. It is not, however, helpful to dump all of this information on someone and then feel as if you have done your job. Very few people will absorb, or be interested in absorbing, all of that information. It is important to be well-informed when talking on these topics, but when referencing facts and sources, it is best to keep these as brief and pointed as possible. If the other person needs clarification or detail, let him or her ask for it.

Do not send them off to some other source

When someone is talking with another person about their faith, and they run up against a challenge, often they will be tempted to refer the person to outside sources. "You should read C.S. Lewis' *Mere Christianity*, he has a really good answer for that question."

In most cases, that person will never read the source to which you refer them. They will, instead, assume that you did not have a good answer and are just making an excuse.

A better approach would be to tell them that you remember a good answer to this, and that you would like to find it and get back to them with that answer. This way, you are doing the work instead of making them do something they probably aren't interested in doing in the first place.

Listening

When you and another person are having a conversation about your faith, you have an opinion and they have an opinion. Both of you probably think that you are right and that the other person is wrong. Consequently, both of you are on a mission to prove your point of view.

In cases like this, each person is usually more interested in asserting his or her view than he or she is in listening to the other person's view. If you are to get the other person to consider your point of view, you need to pay him or her the same courtesy. Moreover, you need to get the other person to really deeply consider *his or her own* opinion. If the other person finds that his or her worldview has some deficiencies, he or she is going to be more willing to hear the solutions your worldview has to offer. In order to do this, there are several techniques worth applying.

Show that you are listening

This involves nodding your head and giving brief responses to what the other is saying, such as "Uh-huh," "Really?" "Got it."

Rephrase what the other person is saying back to them

It helps the other person to feel he or she is being understood to hear you tell him or her back what you heard in your own words. So that if the person says:

"I used to go to church as a kid. My dad had us in the pews each Sunday. He was a deacon in the church and he sang the hymns louder than anyone else there. Then when we came home, he would verbally and physically abuse us."

A good rephrase of this might be:

"So you are saying you don't trust religion because of the way that your religious father acted and treated you?"

This response shows the other person that you understood him or her, and prompts him or her to expand on what he or she was just saying.

By showing the other person that you are truly listening to and absorbing what he or she is saying, you are much more likely to win his or her respect and confidence, two important tools if you want him or her to then consider what you have to say.

Another, *very* important advantage of this method is that it allows you to point out possible flaws in the other person's thought process. For instance:

"I can't believe the Bible. It's barbaric. How am I supposed to like a God that would wipe out the entire earth with a flood? Or command the slaughter of women and children of the Canaanites and the Amalekites?"

"So you are saying that because the Bible is unpleasant that it is also untrue?"

In this example, the Christian has pointed out that whether or not you like something has nothing to do with the truth or falsity of that thing. This causes the nonbeliever to have to rephrase the objection and allows the conversation to go deeper.

Find common ground

It is important when conversing about differing beliefs to highlight every point on which you and the other person agree. The other person probably shares values and beliefs that you regard as well. Here are some examples of how this might be done:

Example 1

Unbeliever: "I can't respect a God that would command the Israelites to slaughter Canaanite women and children in the book of Joshua!"

Believer: "I can definitely agree with you that life is important and that we have an obligation to protect and help those who can't protect themselves."

In this example, the believer has recognized and agreed with the moral impulse of the unbeliever. Rather than jumping into an immediate defense of the Biblical story, the believer has taken time to acknowledge that both he or she and the other person

225

share a common moral instinct; a fact that can later parlay into a reason for the Christian worldview: universal morality.

Example 2

Unbeliever: "Christians take everything on faith. I need facts if I'm going to trust something."

Believer: "That's a smart way to approach things. Without facts, you could be tricked into believing anything."

In this instance, what the unbeliever has offered was a mischaracterization of Christianity. But rather than disagreeing with the first part of the statement, "Christians take everything on faith," the believer agrees with the second part of the statement. Once the common ground has been established, the believer can then offer an alternative definition of "faith" and start to build a factual case for Christianity. A stronger version of the same thing might look like this:

Example 3

Unbeliever: "Christians reject science. Their answer to everything is 'God did it.' They pray to some kind of sky buddy and just blind themselves to the fact that none of their prayers are answered and they are blissfully ignorant to the fact that the world is just getting worse. They look down their noses at everybody around them when they act worse than unbelievers."

Believer: "That does sound ridiculous. If someone told me that is what they believed, I wouldn't agree with it, either."

In this instance, the unbeliever has offered a biased and hostile view of Christian beliefs that paints them as a ridiculous caricature. Rather than being insulted, the believer has agreed that the type of religion they just described is absolutely as ridiculous as it sounds. This will likely take the wind out of the unbeliever's sails, and allow the believer to describe the type of Christianity that they actually practice.

The Power of the Question

Many conversations about faith take place over the internet in this day and age. This kind of conversation has a number of advantages in that it allows people to think about and edit what they are saying to give the best answer possible, *and* to research their answer before they give it.

A face-to-face conversation is far more challenging. Because each person has to say what each wants to say immediately, and to come up with any facts or arguments off the top of each one's head, it is prone to getting emotional, and to leave the believer stumped even if he or she knows there is a good answer.

In both online and face-to-face conversations, asking questions is one of the most powerful and effective tools in defending the faith. It is easy to come up with a question in a conversation, even if it is to ask for the other person to clarify or expand on what he or she has just said. It gives the person asking the question more time to understand and come up with a response. Most importantly, questioning back along the person's line of reasoning helps *him or her* see the deficiencies in his or her own argument. For instance, here is an actual quote from an online conversation on Christianity:

> *Religions are created by men (and I do mean males) because*
> *human fears respecting life experiences and questions on life,*
> *what happens after death, promote the creation of religions*
> *to answer those quandaries. Some prophets were inspired*

and perhaps came in touch with the Infinite Intelligence that has guided some ever since humanity evolved from its simian origins. But that eternal source is within each person and needs no legends, only direct listening, learning and evolving as souls.

In this example, the person is making a number of unsubstantiated claims. It would only be reasonable to ask her how she came by this knowledge. If she is unable to back up her claims with some kind of source facts, she has no grounds upon which to accuse Christianity to be a made-up religion, especially since—as this book has shown—Christianity *does* have a great deal of evidential proof.

Every person holds certain values or opinions. If they didn't, they wouldn't be challenging Christianity. However, if Christianity is true, then those values or opinions that they hold are either ultimately grounded in the existence of the Christian God, or entirely ungrounded.

In order for something to be valuable, it has to be assigned that value by someone. Therefore, if people want you to agree with their values and opinions, they are going to have to show why that thing should be held valuable to you as well as to them.

Let's take one of the examples we looked at above. Say someone used the argument:

"I can't respect a God that would command the Israelites to slaughter Canaanite women and children in the book of Joshua!"

There are two values being expressed here:

1.) Life is valuable
2.) Those unable to defend themselves should receive protection

Both of these values are fairly easy to defend from a Christian perspective. Life is valuable because it is given by God. Life is something that only God can give. Humans cannot manufacture or restore life. Moreover, human life in particular is valuable because humans are created in God's image, giving them a special place in creation. God himself commanded "Thou shalt not murder," making the preservation of human life a fundamental moral law.

In both Old and New Testaments, the protection and care of widows and orphans is mandated. Moreover, parents are given the duty to protect and care for their children and elderly. The protection of the weaker members by the stronger feeds into the first premise—life is valuable—and also reflects the "Love thy neighbor" rule as expressed in the Good Samaritan parable.

Now remove Christianity entirely. How does the person defend the premises that life is valuable and that those unable to defend themselves should receive protection? How can they justify this as something that applies to everyone, everywhere, regardless of culture or personal opinion?

Let's review a potential conversation using the techniques we just discussed (all of the objections to Christianity represented in this conversation are based on actual objections I have encountered):

> **Non-Christian:** "Religions like Christianity were invented to control people. They just feed people a lie that keeps them from thinking for themselves and making their own decisions."

> **Christian:** "So you are saying that Christianity is bad because it deceives people?"

> **Non-Christian:** "Yes. Imagine all of the scientific advancements we would have made if we didn't

have Christianity holding society back telling us that 'God did it' is a sufficient answer."

Christian: "It sounds like you believe that the pursuit of truth is important."

Non-Christian: "It is absolutely important."

Christian: "Why is truth important? Why not simply believe whatever makes you happy?"

In this example, we see that with relatively little work, the Christian has managed to back the non-Christian into a corner. In raising the objection to Christianity, the non-Christian has expressed the essential importance of truth, but he or she has no grounding for that value. On the other hand, the Christian *does* have a grounding for the importance of truth.

All values are ultimately grounded in a Christian God. Questioning a person's values and standards is one of the easiest ways of forcing the person to that realization.

One of the beauties of this technique is that it is very effective in dealing with people who tend to abduct the conversation and then filibuster their opinion, not allowing you to get a word in edgewise. Almost everyone is more interested in talking than in listening. As a result, they are usually far more willing to answer questions than they are to hear your viewpoint. If your questions cause them to realize the deficiencies in their own viewpoint, it can give you the chance to offer your own answer to those same questions.

Don't let them tell you what you believe

In the previous sections, we have seen a number of examples of what philosophers call "straw men." A "straw man" is when another person tells you what you believe and then tells you why this belief is wrong—they set up a straw man so they can knock it down. Some of the examples we have seen are:

"Christians take everything on faith. They just believe things without any evidence."

and

"Christians reject science. Their answer to everything is 'God did it.' They pray to some kind of sky buddy and just blind themselves to the fact that none of their prayers are answered and they are blissfully ignorant to the fact that the world is just getting worse. They look down their noses at everybody around them when they act worse than unbelievers."

It is easy to get caught up defending things that you don't actually believe. It is important to recognize that the characterization of your beliefs that the other person is expressing are not actually what you believe. In an instance like this, it is best to exercise our strategy of agreeing with the opponent:

"That does sound ridiculous. That's not actually what I believe."

This opens the door for the other person to ask what it is that you *do* believe, at which point you may begin to lay out your case and your beliefs.

It is also important that the Christian does not do this in reverse. Allow the other person to tell you what he or she believes, rather than assuming his or her beliefs in order to disprove him or her. It is always far more effective to ask people questions about why they believe what they believe until they have no answers to give, showing that their beliefs are baseless (The Power of the Question).

231

Stay Focused

Conversations on heated topics like politics and religion are prone to wander all over the map. In answering one question or objection, fifty more are raised. Often, the person doesn't even get all the way through his or her answer when the other person interrupts to object to or question a point in the answer, or to loudly voice an opinion on the subject.

Because of this, it is exceptionally easy to get sidetracked and lose any effectiveness the conversation might have otherwise served. Here are some things to keep in mind that are important to keep the conversation focused.

Focus on the argument, not the source

Ostriches are flightless birds. This is a fact. Facts are true regardless of where they come from. If Albert Einstein or Forest Gump says "Ostriches are flightless birds," they are still flightless birds. The same is true for fallacies. *Ostriches can fly* is a fallacy. It doesn't matter who says it, it's not true. No matter how educated or erudite they are, if they say ostriches can fly, they are mistaken.

Quite frequently, people question the truth or falsity of an argument or claim based on the source. You believe Jesus rose from the dead? What do you know? You don't even have a college degree. I know a guy with three doctorates who says Jesus *didn't* rise from the dead.

Whether or not Jesus rose from the dead has nothing to do with who believes it or not. If true, it would continue to be true even if *no one* believed it.

Even an expert in a particular area would have to give a factual explanation for his or her beliefs. For instance, if a Hebrew scholar says that a particular Hebrew document is a forgery, she would then have to give reasons for her findings (the type of paper, the type of ink, the dialect used, etc.).

If a conversation strays into comparing the relative merits of the two people conversing, or quoting a variety of authorities who believe one thing or another, it has gotten off-track, and it proves nothing. The focus must be facts and evidence, not people.

Focus on the topic at hand

As mentioned before, on a topic as controversial and heated as religion, conversations can frequently dive down a variety of rabbit trails without ever going anywhere. For instance, imagine that you are having a conversation with a non-Christian about Jesus' resurrection. You are talking about the New Testament documents, and the person says that there are many contradictions in the documents. You ask for an example, and they bring up the different number of angels that different gospels mention at the tomb. You begin to address this objection, and then the person asks if you believe in angels. You start to defend the existence of angels, and then they argue that the creation of angels is not part of the creation account. You begin to talk about the possible creation of angels, and then the person waylays into an argument against a young earth and a six-day creation. In talking about this, the conversation strays into an argument on evolution. This turns into an argument on science versus faith, which then turns into an argument on historical atrocities associated with the Christian Church.

This type of discussion is far too common. It tends to anger both parties without actually answering any of the questions raised.

There are two types of people who tend to confront Christians with these kinds of questions: those who are genuinely looking for an answer, and those who are only looking to pick a fight.

It is very helpful to identify with which type of person you are dealing, because it will do a great deal to direct your approach.

If the person with whom you are conversing has genuine questions about Christian beliefs, then it is in both of your best interests to give these questions serious consideration and answer them as best as you are able. This might involve telling them that you need to look into their question more deeply and get back to them, but whatever you do, be certain to give the question the effort it deserves.

Since a person like this is liable to have many questions about Christianity, the person is just as likely as anyone else to raise new questions and challenges as you attempt to answer the original question. However, this kind of person is also more likely to respect you when you ask if you can finish this answer before you begin another.

If it is helpful, make a list of the questions the person has, and address each one in turn. However, it is essential to stay focused on the one answer before moving on to others.

The second type of person—the one just looking to start a fight—isn't interested in hearing answers to the questions, and less interested in hearing a convincing argument. Challenging everything you have to say is just part of this person's tactic, and he or she is unlikely to respect you if you ask to be able to finish one answer before moving on to the next. Assuming that you can get the person to listen to any one of your answers, it is still unlikely that he or she is going to be swayed.

For this type of person, a separate tactic can be effective.

The "Refocusing" Tactic

Over the centuries, Christians have argued over practically every aspect of their beliefs. The massive amount of disagreement that Christians have undergone has caused Christians to ask "What are the essential facts you would *have to* believe in order to call yourself a Christian?"

Like most other things, different Christians will offer different answers to the question; however, a general consensus can be had that at least the resurrection and deity of Jesus - the points we have argued in this book - are essentials to faith.

The *Refocusing* tactic encourages a person to select a few essential points upon which his or her faith stands or falls, and focus *only on those points.*

This is not to say that other aspects of the faith are unimportant, but it *does* mean that one can be saved without necessarily embracing or even being aware of all aspects of Christian teachings.

Imagine for a moment that a Christian begins talking to a Muslim woman on an airplane ride. The Christian and the Muslim agree that God is judgmental toward sins. The Christian shares that God doesn't simply ask people to perform in order to achieve favor, but actually offers unconditional forgiveness through Christ Jesus, his death, and his resurrection.

Having never heard a Gospel of forgiveness before, the Muslim woman is convicted, kneels, and offers her life to Christ.

Most Christians would generally agree that she is, at that point, "saved." They would also agree that she brings a lot of Islamic baggage with her that would need to be worked out as she learns about her new faith, but the most important step has already been taken.

At the start, this book put forth the thesis that *External Apologetics* should be primarily evangelical in nature. That is to say that any discussion of Christianity between a Christian and a non-Christian should be done with the goal of sharing the Gospel with the nonbeliever, causing him or her to have to make a decision. Evangelism is not—and never has been—about training the other person in all the nuances of Christianity, nor answering every question one can possibly come up with. It is about convincing one of the need for a savior, and then supplying the person with a savior.

Once this has been accomplished, it is the job of *Internal Apologetics* to answer all of the questions this untrained believer might have about the faith.

Christianity is a worldview that, if true, *demands* a decision from people. To convince someone of the truth of Christianity without any call to embrace the salvation it offers is pointless.

Seeing as the point of the conversation is to convince the other person of the basic truth of the Gospel, there are a lot of points that *do not need* to be argued.

From the beginning, this book has made the case that the life, death, and resurrection of Jesus should be the main focus of *External Apologetics*. To this end, if a person begins to make an objection to Christian ideas that do not directly relate to the person of Christ, it is within the best interest of the Christian to *redirect* the conversation.

Redirecting works in one of two ways: either it uses the point raised in order to bring the conversation back around to Jesus, or it points out that the objection does not defeat the basic truth of Christianity.

The first approach will only work in certain situations, and only with some considerate thought. For instance, if someone raises the question "If God is good, why is there so much suffering in the world?" the response could bring the person back around to the Gospel like this:

> "Well, give me a specific example of suffering in the world."

> "What about the thousands of people dying of AIDS in Africa?"

> "So you're saying that if God were to eliminate AIDS in Africa, you would be satisfied that he is good?"

> "No, of course not! There is all kinds of suffering besides just AIDS in Africa!"

"Okay, so let's say that God eliminated all disease everywhere. Would this solve your objection?"

"Disease isn't the only problem, what about earthquakes and hurricanes?"

"Well, let's say that God eliminated all forms of natural evil. In fact, let's say that God eliminated death entirely, and everyone lived forever, would that solve the problem?"

"I guess, maybe."

"And you're not concerned with things like abuse, neglect, and rape?"

"Okay, yeah, there you go! That's another type of suffering that people have!"

"Okay, so you are saying that God would somehow need to change human nature from doing evil things, AND offer eternal life in order to be good?"

"Yeah."

"That's exactly what he does through Jesus Christ."

If a person is creative, many such objections can be brought back around to the Gospel, but it is not always possible in a brief conversation to think of ways to do this. This is why the second tactic is important.

In what we will call *surrendering the point*, the Christian does not attempt to answer the objection. Rather, he or she simply points out that even if the objection is valid, it does not defeat the basic point of salvation through Jesus' death and resurrection.

For instance, if someone were to challenge the Christian by pointing out that the story of Jonah and the whale is complete mythology, and that there is no way a human could survive three days inside a fish's stomach, the Christian can simply respond, "Let's say you're right. How does this disprove Christianity?"

"It proves the Bible has errors."

"Again, for the sake of argument, let's say the Bible has some errors. We still have good reason to believe that Jesus rose from the dead. And if Jesus rose from the dead, Christianity remains true, despite whatever errors you may or may not find in other parts of scripture."

Once the conversation has been redirected to Jesus' resurrection, the material discussed in this book becomes the Apologetic grounds upon which the Christian can make the case for Christ.

In this way, you are not admitting that you *believe* the objection is valid, you are simply stating that it is irrelevant in terms of salvation.

Chapter 20
CONCLUSION

In this book, we have looked at the difference between *Internal* and *External* apologetics. We have made the case that External Apologetics should be primarily evangelical in nature. To that end, we have attempted to examine a comprehensive case for Jesus and his resurrection.

In order to do so, we have firstly examined the documents claiming to report on Jesus' life, teachings, death, and resurrection. We have made the case that the New Testament documents that contain this information were written early—within decades of the events. We have then examined the eyewitness nature of the documents, first by looking at each gospel individually, and then by looking at how they support one another in their details. We have made the case that the New Testament that we have today is accurate based on the document evidence. We have looked at external evidence for the truth of the New Testament documents, including secular writings of the day and archeological finds. We have looked at the bare minimal facts that the most liberal scholars will accept as true, and from those built the case that Jesus did, indeed, rise from the dead.

After looking at the New Testament, we then took a foray into the Old Testament, looking at predictions that it made about the Messiah and how Jesus matched those predictions.

Finally, we have examined a few strategies for relating this information to non-Christians in an effective way, including:

1.) Be nice (say I'm not attacking you)
2.) Don't do an information dump
3.) Listen (active listening)
4.) Ask questions (presuppositional apologetics)
5.) Don't let them tell you what you believe
6.) Stay focused on:
    a. The issue, not the person
    b. The topic at hand
       i. Redirection technique
    c. The Gospel

Apologeticsindex.org defines 'apologetics' as "the branch of Christian theology concerned with the intelligent presentation and defense of the historical Christian faith."

In his book, *Apologetics Never Saved Anyone*, Dr. Fred DeRuvo characterizes the practice of Apologetics as so much noisy debate that does nothing but to inflate the ego of the Apologist and to incite resentment in the person being argued with.

This is a fairly common objection within the Christian community.

For those Christians who oppose the practice of Apologetics, their argument is this: the job of the church is to preach the Gospel—that is, to tell people about their rebellion against God and the forgiveness purchased by Christ Jesus at the cross. It is this message that saves, not arguing facts with people.

There are two reasons why Apologetics remains a useful practice, even in light of this objection.

The first reason is that there are many truly devoted Christians who struggle with their questions and with the intellectual and emotional bullying and abuse that they receive regarding their faith from the political and academic realms. These Christians hunger for a more rigorous structure of reason to justify their beliefs. Apologetics is growing in popularity within the Church, not within the University or the Senate. Believers benefit when they can comfortably found their faith within reason.

In fact, one of the main objections of the New Atheists is that they feel that religious faith is unreasonable, and can lead to unreasonable actions and practices. In his February 2011 article in *The Nation*, Peter Filicietti nicely encapsulates this objection when he states:

> "The faith that religion relies on and enforces is blind faith, which is why, being wholly divorced from reason and evidence, religion tends to favour inquisitions and blasphemy charges to maintain the faith. Opening itself to free speech, rational criticism, and verifiable observation would not be conducive to maintaining a stranglehold on the blinded faithful."

So even they who disbelieve must admit that it is far better for a religious group to apply reason and logic to their beliefs then to just blindly believe. Since both Christians and Atheists are convinced of the truthfulness of their own position, neither should suffer any fear of applying the light of reason to their ideals.

The Bible commands believers to examine and explore their own faith, so that even if not one single soul is brought to repentance through Apologetic argumentation, it is still of deep benefit to the established believer.

Secondly, Apologetics and Evangelism can, in fact, be reconciled into a single message. That message would go something like this:

Two thousand years ago, there was a real, historical figure who claimed that he was God. When this man was asked for a sign that his claims were true, he replied that when they destroyed his body, he would raise it back to life in three days. They destroyed his body. He raised it back to life in three days. In so doing, he verified his claim, confirming the existence of God and delivering the Gospel message.

Jesus' resurrection is both the salvation of the Evangelist and the evidence of the Apologist.

BIBLIOGRAPHY

I am greatly indebted to the following sources for the material presented in this book:

J. Warner Wallace for providing several illustrations from his apologetic work and police career; for laying out the argument for *The Gospel of Mark* being based on the teachings of the Apostle Peter in a personal interview; and for the external historical references to Christianity provided in his book, *Cold Case Christianity*.

Dr. Tim McGrew for the invaluable consultations on historical evidence, and especially for his work on answering the historical objections to *The Gospel of Luke.*

Dr. Daniel Wallace for his case for the formation and transmission of the New Testament Documents.

Dr. Gary Habermas for his extensive work and development of the "Minimal Facts Approach."

[1] Lewis, C.S. (1952) *Mere Christianity*

[2] Sagan, Carl (1980) *Cosmos*

[3] "Temple, The Second" (1901-1906), *Jewish Encyclopedia*

[4] Josephus, Flavius, *Complete Works of Flavius Josephus: Wars of the Jews, Antiquities of the Jews, Against Apion, Autobiography,*

trans. William Whiston (Boston: MobileReference), Kindle edition, Kindle locations 7243-7249

[5] Simmons, Shraga. (Retrieved May/20/13) "Tisha B'Av – Ninth of Av"

[6] Josephus, Flavius *Complete Works of Flavius Josephus*, Kindle locations 28589 – 28592

[7] Clarke, Adam, *Adam Clarke's Commentary on the Bible* (Grand Rapids, MI: Baker, 1983), commenting on Acts 28:31

[8] Aune, David (2010) *The Blackwell Companion to The New Testament*, pg. 9

[9] Wallace, J. Warner (2013) *Cold-Case Christianity*, pg. 164

[10] Wallace, J. Warner (2013) pg. 165

[11] Bruce, F.F. (1984) *The New Testament Documents: Are They Reliable?* (Downers Grove, IL: InterVarsity Press), Kindle edition, Kindle location 409.

[12] MacArthur, John (2005) *The MacArthur Bible Commentary*, pg. 1111

[13] Brown, R., (1994) *The death of the Messiah,* vol. I, Doubleday, New York. Pg. 299

[14] MacArthur, John (2005) pg. 1188

[15] MacArthur, John (2005) pg. 1264

[16] MacArthur, John (2005) pg. 1338

[17] Peters, F.E. (2009) *The Quest: The Historians' Search for Jesus and Muhammad* (Recorded Book Edition; The Modern Scholar)

[18] Black, Ellen Lowrie (2008) "Apostle John: Chosen as a Teen" Association of Christian Schools International Youth Leadership Convention. Palmer, AK.

[19] Saint Sophronius of Jerusalem (2007) "The Life of the Evangelist John", *The Explanation of the Holy Gospel According to John,* House Springs, Missouri, USA: Chrysostom Press, pp. 2-3, ISBN 1-889814-09-1

[20] MacArthur, John (2005) pg. 1339

[21] Wallace, Daniel B. (2004) "Matthew: Introduction, Argument, and Outline," retrieved 1/17/2014 from https://bible.org/seriespage/matthew-introduction-argument-and-outline

[22] *Fragments of Papias* 2:16, Daniel Wallace, translator.

[23] Wallace, J. Warner (2013) "Is Mark's Gospel an Early Memoir of the Apostle Peter?" retrieved 1/17/2014 from http://coldcasechristianity.com/2014/is-marks-gospel-an-early-memoir-of-the-apostle-peter/

[24] Brown, Raymond E. (1997). *Introduction to the New Testament.* New York: Anchor Bible. pg. 164

[25] Helms, Randel McCraw (1997) *Who Wrote the Gospels?*

[26] Eusebius, *Ecclesiastical History* 6.14.5-7

[27] Aland, Kurt; Barbara Aland; Erroll F. Rhodes (trans.) (1995). *The Text of the New Testament: An Introduction to the Critical Editions and to the Theory and Practice of Modern Textual Criticism.* Grand Rapids: William B. Eerdmans Publishing Company. p. 99. ISBN 978-0-8028-4098-1.

[28] Wallace, J. Warner (2013) *Cold-Case Christianity,* pg. 167

[29] McGrew, Timothy (2012) "Alleged Historical Errors in the Gospels, Part 1" audio resource: http://www.apologetics315.com/2012/11/audio-resources-by-tim-mcgrew.html

[30] *The Shepherd of Hermas* 1:1-5, J.B. Lightfoot, translator.

[31] Josephus, Flavius, *Antiquities of the Jews* (XX:6:3),

[32] Ramsay, Sir William (1915) *The Bearing of Recent Discovery on the Trustworthiness of the New Testament,* pg. 222

[33] Neil, Stephen (1964) *The Interpretation of the New Testament: 1861-1961,* London: Oxford University press, p.143).

[34] McGrew, Timothy (2012) "Alleged Historical Errors in the Gospels, Part 2" audio resource: http://www.apologetics315.com/2012/11/audio-resources-by-tim-mcgrew.html

[35] Bruce, Frederick Fyvie (2003) *The New Testament Documents, Are They Reliable?* Pg. 87

[36] McRay, John (1991) *Archaeology and the New Testament,* pg. 154

[37] Ray, Steve (?) "Gospel of Luke: Greek Physician, Historian & Friend of Mary," retrieved 1/17/2014 from http://www.catholic-convert.com/wp-content/uploads/Documents/003Luke.pdf

[38] Bunch, Taylor G. (1940), *Behold the Man*, Pacific Press Publishing Association (Mountain View, California, USA), p.59

[39] Robert M. Price (2003) *The Incredible Shrinking Son of Man* p. 14

[40] James F. Strange and Hershel Shanks (1983), "Synagogue Where Jesus Preached Found at Capernaum," Biblical Archaeology Review 9

[41] Ehrman, Bart D. (2009), *Jesus, Interrupted.* Harper Collins

[42] MacDonald, William (1995) *Believer's Bible Commentary*, pg. 1463

[43] MacDonald, William (1995) pg. 1464

[44] Wallace, J. Warner (2013) pgs. 74-75

[45] Hannah, Dr. John D. (2001) *Our Legacy*, pgs. 38-40

[46] Hannah, Dr. John D. (2001) pgs. 44-

[47] Kruger, Michael (2013) "Ten Basic Facts About the NT Canon That Every Christian Should Memorize: The Apocryphal Books Were Written in the Second Century or Later," retrieved 1/23/2014 from http://michaeljkruger.com/ten-basic-facts-about-the-nt-canon-that-every-christian-should-memorize-2-apocryphal-writings-areall-written-in-the-second-century-or-later/

[48] Kruger, Michael (2013) "Ten Basic Facts About the NT Canon That Every Christian Should Memorize: At the End of the Second Century, the Muratorian Fragment Lists 22 of our 27 NT Books," retrieved 1/23/2014 from http://michaeljkruger.com/ten-basic-facts-about-the-nt-canon-that-every-christian-should-memorize-6-at-the-end-of-the-second-century-the-muratorian-fragment-lists-22-of-our-27-nt-books-2/

[49] Kruger, Michael (2013) "Ten Basic Facts About the NT Canon That Every Christian Should Memorize: Early Christians

Often Used Noncanonical Writings," retrieved 1/23/2014 from http://michaeljkruger.com/ten-basic-facts-about-the-nt-canon-that-every-christian-should-memorize-7-early-christians-often-used-noncanonical-writings/

[50] Kruger, Michael (2013) "Ten Basic Facts About the NT Canon That Every Christian Should Memorize: The NT Canon Was Not Decided at Nicea – Nor Any Other Church Council," retrieved 1/23/2014 from http://michaeljkruger.com/ten-basic-facts-about-the-nt-canon-that-every-christian-should-memorize-8-the-nt-canon-was-not-decided-at-nicea-nor-any-other-church-council/

[51] Wallace, Dr. Daniel B. (2013) Lecture "How Badly Did Scribes Change the New Testament?" retrieved 1/23/2014 from http://www.youtube.com/watch?v=b-RMdX0zi-Q

[52] MacArthur, John (2005), pgs. 1261-1262

[53] Parker, David (2012) "Codex Bezae," retrieved 2/28/2014 from http://cudl.lib.cam.ac.uk/view/MS-NN-00002-00041/1

[54] MacArthur, John (2005) pg. 1383

[55] MacArthur, John (2005) pg. 1967

[56] Wallace, J. Warner (2013) pgs. 192-193

[57] Pines, Shlomo (1971) *An Arabic Version of the Testimonium Flavianum and Its Implications* (Israel Academy of Sciences and Humanities: Jerusalem) Kindle Edition, Kindle locations 9-10, 16

[58] Quoted in *Anti-Nicene Christian Library: Translations of the Writings of the Fathers Down to A.D. 325,* eds. Alexander Roberts and James Donaldson, vol. 9, *Irenaeus, Vol. II – Hippolytus, Vol. II – Fragments of Third Century* (Edinburgh: T & T Clark, 1870), 188

[59] Quoted in *Ante-Nicene Christian Library,* eds. Roberts and Donaldson, vol. 9, 188

[60] "Letter from Mara Bar-Serapion to His Son," quoted in Bruce, *New Testament Documents,* Kindle locations 1684-1688

[61] Origen, "Origen Against Celsus," *The Ante-Nicene Fathers*, eds. Alexander Roberts and James Donaldson, vol. 4, *Tertullian, Part Fourth; Minucius Felix; Commodian; Origen, Parts First and Second* (Buffalo: Christian Literature, 1885), 437, 445, 455

[62] Habermas, Gary (2012) "The Minimal Facts Approach to the Resurrection of Jesus: The Role of Methodology as a Crucial Component in Establishing Historicity," retrieved 3/3/14 from http://www.garyhabermas.com/articles/southeastern_theo logical_review/minimal-facts-methodology_08-02-2012.htm